THE *Sol e Mar* TRAGEDY
OFF MARTHA'S VINEYARD

CAPTAIN W. RUSSELL WEBSTER, USCG (RET.)
& ELIZABETH B. WEBSTER

Foreword by Rear Admiral George Naccara, USCG (Ret.)

THE
History
PRESS

Published by The History Press
Charleston, SC 29403
www.historypress.net

Copyright © 2014 by Captain W. Russell Webster and Elizabeth B. Webster
All rights reserved

Front cover, map: Courtesy of the Norman B. Leventhal Map Center at the Boston Public Library.

First published 2014

ISBN 978.1.5402.2359.3

Library of Congress CIP data applied for.

Notice: The information in this book is true and complete to the best of our knowledge. It is offered without guarantee on the part of the authors or The History Press. The authors and The History Press disclaim all liability in connection with the use of this book.

All rights reserved. No part of this book may be reproduced or transmitted in any form whatsoever without prior written permission from the publisher except in the case of brief quotations embodied in critical articles and reviews.

This book is dedicated to William "Hokey" Hokanson and Billy Hokanson, who died doing what they loved most—fishing—on the night of March 25, 1990, off Martha's Vineyard. May your memories live on in the dreams of your loved ones.

Hokey and Billy share a tender moment in the *Sol e Mar* wheelhouse, circa 1985. *Image courtesy of Ellen (Hokanson) Ouellette.*

CONTENTS

Foreword, by Rear Admiral George Naccara   7
Preface   9
Acknowledgements   15

1. "Hokey" and Billy   19
2. Domestic Terrorism: Anatomy of Hoax Callers   37
3. "We're Sinking, We Need Help Now!"   45
4. *Sol e Mar* Investigations   53
5. Next of Kin (NOK) Procedures   75
6. The Studds Act and Hoax Calls Past and Present   81
7. The Coast Guard's Technology in 1990 and Now   89
8. Human Factors and Decision Making   97
9. Connections to the Past   105

Postscript   111
Bibliography   119
Index   123
About the Authors   128

FOREWORD

Emergency responders know teenagers and young adults make the most phony distress calls, but some older adults with darker motivations actively mislead first responders, too. With certainty, these deliberate and misleading calls on open radio frequencies, cellphones and even landlines misdirect search efforts, prolong the search, endanger rescuers and often seal the fates of those actually in distress.

Until we have more sophisticated equipment with which the Coast Guard (or any emergency responder) could immediately identify a transmission source by location or electronic signature, the question of stopping hoax calls remains unanswered. Technology, however, may provide only a partial solution, since it may be impossible to regulate and rectify some human behaviors.

In the tragic case of the sinking of the *Sol e Mar* off Martha's Vineyard on March 25, 1990, no rescue units were launched for several days until the vessel carrying "Hokey" Hokanson (forty-four) and his son, Billy (nineteen), was reported overdue. The Coast Guard believed their garbled distress call was connected to the hoax call that immediately followed, and later analysis would determine that the malicious prank caller had been on land in the Woods Hole, Massachusetts area, transmitting on a low-power radio.

In a groundbreaking book, historian Captain W. Russ Webster, U.S. Coast Guard (Ret.), a leading international expert on search and rescue (SAR) cases, and Elizabeth Webster, a longtime print journalist, explore the *Sol e Mar* tragedy for the first time. This book will soon become essential reading

Foreword

for understanding hoax cases previously found in only dry, uninspiring formal investigations conducted by federal agencies. Repeated technological limitations and the failures associated with the primary mission of the U.S. Coast Guard are the focus of complex but engaging analyses. In vivid terms, the Websters detail remarkable improvements in the methods and equipment the Coast Guard has implemented in recent years as rescuers attempt to take the "search" out of the term "search and rescue."

The authors deftly analyze accounts of fishermen, family members and technical experts involved in the *Sol e Mar* case, some of whom heard the actual distress call. They explore why people prank, what they seek in the action and the extraordinary cost in lives lost and resources expended caused by hoax calls. Their unique work also paints the mosaic of the main characters and fishermen victims. After reading the Websters' narration of who these men were, you will understand why many people in the Cape Cod and Fairhaven area still miss these vibrant, colorful characters.

As a former field commander of Coast Guard District One (which covers the area from Canada to Toms River, New Jersey) with an extensive marine safety background in operations ashore and afloat and as the former chief information officer for the service, I have witnessed firsthand the deadly effects of prank calls all too often. The effect on my former service's capability to respond when we were already operating on extremely tight budgets, the risk to responders themselves and the cost to taxpayers was and is unacceptable.

As the former TSA federal security director of Massachusetts with multimodal transportation responsibilities, I wrote this foreword because the contents of this book resonated with my values, and the extensive research conducted to bring this topic to life merits a deep immersion into the topic. The result is a high-quality product appropriate for educators and students of search and rescue, mariners of all types and the general-interest reader.

You will literally fly through this eminent and readable book, and the words of Jim Loy, former commandant of the Coast Guard, will assuredly echo: "We show the greatest respect for those who have been lost—especially for those who die unnecessarily—when we use the occasion of their deaths to prevent others from sharing their fates."

Rear Admiral George Naccara
U.S. Coast Guard (Ret.)
Former Commander
First Coast Guard District

PREFACE

On the evening of March 25, 1990, William "Hokey" Hokanson (forty-four) and his son, Billy Hokanson (nineteen), died lonely deaths as their fishing vessel, the *Sol e Mar* ("Sun and Sea" in Portuguese) flooded and sank for unknown reasons.

Young Billy was able to get off only a four-second, heavily garbled cry for help over the radio. Within one minute and twenty seconds after young Billy's call, a hoax caller—a modern-day terrorist—would confuse Coast Guard rescuers into believing he was Billy Hokanson. Despite enough clues to indicate there were two calls, no rescue assets would be dispatched until five days later, when a family member reported the *Sol e Mar* overdue.

The case prompted then Massachusetts congressman Gerry Studds to sponsor a tough new anti-hoax law that would see convicted hoax callers face up to six years in prison and $250,000 in civil penalties, plus bear the burden of the costs of the rescue effort. Despite the new law and several subsequent successful prosecutions, the Coast Guard continues to receive an increasing and unacceptable number of radio hoax calls twenty-four years after the *Sol e Mar* sinking.

This book was written because no record of the *Sol e Mar* tragedy exists with the Coast Guard's historian, despite the significance of the case in service history. Additionally, we hope this book will provide an enduring memorialization of the men Hokey and Billy Hokanson were. Their tragic loss at sea at such young ages continues to deeply affect many of their friends and family members in the Fairhaven, Islands and Cape Cod areas of

Preface

Massachusetts. We also intend to chronicle "related lessons learned" so that future Coast Guardsmen may learn from their predecessors' mistakes and judgment calls and mariners may have the best possible chance of survival in an unforgiving environment.

From 1998 to 2001, I was the commander of Coast Guard Group Woods Hole and was responsible for overseeing approximately 1,200 search and rescue (SAR) cases every year. Group Woods Hole, now known as Sector Southeastern New England, is located on Cape Cod in the town of Falmouth's small village of Woods Hole. Much happened there during my tour, despite its rural, bucolic geography.

In my years as Group Woods Hole commander, several tragic high-profile cases earned national attention. I was the incident commander for Coast Guard operations after the July 16, 1999 tragic crash of John F. Kennedy Jr.'s small, private plane seven miles southwest of Martha's Vineyard and the October 31, 1999 Egypt Air Flight 990 in which all 217 persons aboard perished after crashing in waters about sixty miles south of Nantucket.

I was also the Coast Guard's chief of operations for the First Coast Guard District, which covers the northeastern United States (from the Canadian border to Toms River, New Jersey), from 2001 through 2003, during which time I had broad oversight of more than ten thousand search and rescue cases, the execution of traditional missions and the codevelopment of expanded homeland security efforts after the 9/11 terrorist attacks.

One kernel of the idea for this book began during my time as the Group Woods Hole rescue commander from 1998 to 2001 after I corresponded with Cheryl Best, daughter of fisherman William (Hokey) Hokanson, skipper of the fishing vessel *Sol e Mar*, and sister of Billy Hokanson.

The *Sol e Mar* is presumed to have sunk (for reasons that were never officially determined) on the night of March 25, 1990. Knowing that Cheryl Best's dad and brother had died in 1990, at least partially because of a hoax caller, I enlisted her help in 2000 to hallmark the tenth anniversary of the *Sol e Mar* tragedy by being part of a *Cape Cod Times* newspaper article, "Lost in the Waves," on the sinking. I also needed her support for a new Massachusetts state law that would fill a gap in the application of Congressman Gerry Studds's hoax enforcement act that referred juveniles, the main perpetrators of maritime hoax calls, to the state court system. These calls struck fear in decision-makers' minds and consumed a healthy percentage of my rescue crews' energies, risking their lives and distracting them from mariners who were legitimately in trouble in an unforgiving environment.

Preface

In 1998, when I arrived at Group Woods Hole, the Coast Guard was still recovering from manpower shortages from its most recent "streamlining" initiative, which had the service at its smallest size in more than thirty years. Many leaders, including then commandant James Loy, believed we had sufficiently trimmed the fat and expanded our mission set so extensively that we were digging into the muscle and bone of our organization and its sailors. We were doing more with less to the point that we were doing everything with nothing—and all of it was on the shoulders of our young men and women. At the time I took over at Woods Hole, the Coast Guard was also behind schedule in implementing its long-touted $300 million replacement of the network of National Distress System (NDS) VHF-FM transmitters and receivers along the coast. These systems were the radios that Billy Hokanson used and the same systems that today provide the bread-and-butter "tripwire" for mariners issuing radio distress calls within twenty miles of the coast. There were some sixty-eight known "black hole" radio coverage gaps in the NDS's nationwide network in 1998. Chief among those gaps was a radio coverage area off Nomans Island near Martha's Vineyard where the fishing vessel *Sol e Mar* had sunk on March 25, 1990. An admiral and a congressman had called for enhancements to these radio systems in 1990, after the fishing vessel *Sol e Mar* sank in the area of my command. Because of the complex machinations of budget and politics, that particular radio coverage black hole, remarkably, still remained in 1998 when I took command of Group Woods Hole. Moreover, that coverage gap was not a higher priority than any of the other sixty-seven black holes in the system, despite the fact that two lives had been lost and the problem recognized eight years before. As the regional group commander, a historian and one of the Coast Guard's professional "communicators," I made it one of my goals to identify the limits of radio coverage in the area off Nomans Island, where *Sol e Mar* sank, and apply a fix to the problem. Coast Guard volunteer auxiliarists documented the radio coverage gap through painstaking accounting of methodical radio grid surveys, driving their boats back and forth for hours chronicling problem areas. They ably did this and further documented coverage gaps. Eventually, an extra antenna from the Nobska (Woods Hole area) was moved to Peaked Hill on Martha's Vineyard in 2000 to enhance communications in the area where *Sol e Mar* sank.

It was an incomplete fix but an improvement. Now, in 2014, twenty-four years after the *Sol e Mar* tragedy, the Coast Guard has finalized its Rescue 21 project (NDS's successor) in the Group Woods Hole (now Sector Southeastern New England) area that includes the area off Nomans Island.

Preface

Between the Rescue 21 technology and a greater emphasis on protocol and command center management, the Coast Guard is in a better position to document calls as hoaxes. However, the number of hoax calls, year after year since data was collected in 1990, continues to increase.

As my time at the Group Woods Hole progressed, it became clear that almost one-third of all calls that the Coast Guard responded to were probably prank calls, and a good number of those calls were likely made by juveniles. The Studds Act, named for late congressman Gerry E. Studds, was passed in November 1990 in response to the *Sol e Mar* case. The act made making false distress calls a Class D felony and subjected the convicted hoax caller to as much as six years' prison time and steep civil penalties. It also made hoax callers responsible for restitution to the Coast Guard for the cost of the search. The Studds Act, however, was an ineffective legal remedy for cases involving juveniles. There would be no federal jail time or civil penalties for these young suspects, according to Coast Guard lawyers; their cases would just defer to the appropriate state law or their lawyers would negotiate community service time—these were the only options for resolution.

I won't ever forget the father of a young Cape Cod teen who asked me to postpone his son's first weekend of community service with the same operations center watch standers he had attempted to mislead with his father's VHF radio. The father was imploring me to reschedule his son's first session in order for the teen to participate in a local regatta. Needless to say, the teen did his time according to the original schedule.

As a maritime historian, I had embraced my command's rich regional history, including the ill-fated voyage of the *Sol e Mar*; the deaths of Ms. Best's half brother and father attributable to watch personnel's failure to follow Coast Guard procedures; inadequate radio equipment; radio coverage gaps; and the vicious, untimely interjections of a radio hoaxster who confused rescuers into dismissing young Billy Hokanson's true cry for help. But the *Sol e Mar* tragedy was just a local story with lessons that had no wider distribution, for the most part, within the Coast Guard beyond the Group Woods Hole boundaries and teaching aids at the Yorktown, Virginia Search and Rescue School.

There was and still remains no historical record of the *Sol e Mar* rescue case at Coast Guard headquarters with the service's historian. It is our fervent hope that this book will provide an enduring case study and a reference point for responders about the *Sol e Mar* tragedy such that no mariner will have to die unnecessarily and in the manner that the Hokansons did in the cold

Preface

waters off Martha's Vineyard. We also pray that the 1990 radio hoax caller finds the strength to make apologies for his decades-old transgression.

We would also like this book to give some measure of peace to the family members and friends whose relationships were never the same after the loss of Billy and Hokey Hokanson. Their family members have recently begun to repair the damage that was done.

Those with ties to Hokey and Billy have been pivotal to our understanding of the men they were and the enduring memories they created.

CAPTAIN W. RUSSELL WEBSTER
U.S. COAST GUARD (RET.)

ACKNOWLEDGEMENTS

First and foremost, I must acknowledge my coauthor and wife, Elizabeth, for her constant encouragement, for helping with the important book and chapter naming and layout, for her interview skills and for her support, which crystallized the intent and purpose of an otherwise disorganized effort. Her suggestion to coauthor a book during the 2013 federal furlough was a bold gambit but proved again that she is the smarter of the two of us.

Our special thanks to Ellen and Eddie Ouellette for opening their hearts and souls about Hokey and Billy Hokanson to two strangers. Your love and commitment was obvious as we sifted through underwater footage of the *Sol e Mar* wreckage area, home movies, scrapbooks and personal journals detailing who your family was and is. Thank you. May you have solace in knowing many more people will know Hokey and Billy better now that this tragic story has finally been told.

We also want to say thank you to:

Cheryl Best and Randy Oliveira for providing access to their memories. Your early help allowed us to paint the picture of your father, brother, "cousins" and friends and solidified our commitment to telling this story.

Ray and Joyce Oliveira for inviting us into their home, sharing memories and helping us better understand Hokey and Billy.

Fisherman Dave Butcher, skipper of the fishing vessel *Resolute* and the last person to see the Hokansons alive, for sharing stories of his friendship with Hokey and Billy.

Acknowledgements

Fishermen Tim Powers, Dave Dutra and Joe Francis for their stories about their time with the Hokansons.

Jeannie Berberian, Hokey's girlfriend and companion during his last ten months, for providing a better understanding of her lost loved ones.

Jeff Linberg and Dick Searles for their insights into the search for the wreck of the *Sol e Mar*.

Franny Davis, Hokey's good friend, for sharing some great stories.

Mark Forest, friend and former Cape and Islands liaison to Congressmen Gerry Studds and Bill Delahunt, for his help in understanding Congressman Studds's mindset in 1990 toward hoax callers and fishermen in general.

Joe Mokry from the Cape Elizabeth Water Extrication Team for his incredible insights during extreme rescue circumstances and the harmful effects of hoax calls during a difficult rescue.

My friend Commander Michael DaPonte, U.S. Coast Guard, one of my former Group Portland (Maine) duty officers and, later, Group Charleston's command duty officer on the day of the 1997 *Morning Dew* case used as a comparative case in this book. Mike was a key supporter of the intent and research for this book and provided key insights and clarifications throughout the writing process.

My friend fellow maritime historian and past coauthor Theresa Mitchell Barbo for her sound editorial suggestions, constant encouragement and cogent advice. My writing would occur most often on my regular bus trips to and from Boston and Portland, Maine, and when I traveled near and far for the Federal Emergency Management Agency. Partial book chapters, concepts and ideas submitted to my fellow author on one day more often than not were analyzed within a few hours with suggestions for improvement. And in the final weeks and days of this book, her inestimable editing, indexing and style guidance were critical.

Captain John Kondratowicz, U.S. Coast Guard, 2014 sector commander, Sector South Southeast (SSE). Sector SSE includes the former Group Woods Hole area of responsibility where the *Sol e Mar* sank. John was my former Group Woods Hole operations officer and a key advocate for the book. He and his staff provided extraordinary support through the FOIA process, ensuring information was accurate and timely.

Sector SSE's Lieutenant Bryan Swintek for his terrific SAR insights, energy and confidence in current techniques and capabilities. Today's Coast Guard is a better place as a result of your commitment to excellence and professionalism.

My good friend Dr. Peter Smith, who helped me better understand post-traumatic stress when we both worked in South Portland, Maine.

Acknowledgements

Peter's southern Maine EMS organization helped me recognize that rescuers can be victims too when an Air Med helicopter crashed in Casco Bay, Maine, killing a patient and two crew members and affecting local rescue teams significantly.

Drs. Richard Lumb and Ron Breazeale for their friendship and cogent insights and comments in the "Domestic Terrorists: Anatomy of a Hoax Caller" chapter.

Coast Guard historians Bill Thiesen, Scott Price and Bob Browning for their unwavering support and responsiveness.

Master Chief Jack Downey, U.S. Coast Guard (Ret.), former Coast Guard ancient keeper and rescuer of more than seven hundred distressed mariners for his friendship and assistance in finding other credible sources for this book.

Master Chief Tim Pitts, U.S. Coast Guard (Ret.), for helping find credible sources for this book.

Rear Admiral Al Steinman, Public Health Service (Ret.), for his friendship and extraordinary willingness to provide cogent input to critical sections detailing the effects of hypothermia on the mind and body. Dr. Steinman and I previously worked together on a Mishap Analysis Board in March 2000, when Coast Guardsmen lost their lives in a boating accident operating from Coast Guard Station Niagara, New York.

Captain John Astley, U.S. Coast Guard (Ret.), for his extraordinary support in unraveling the convoluted legal details regarding the Studds Act and its applicability to juveniles and for the several conversations that helped a hapless colleague understand nuance in law and write about it.

Coast Guard colleagues Captain Rick "Iron Man" Hartman and Captain Arn "BBA" Heggers for being good friends and providing me support and technical advice.

Dr. Carlos Comperatore for his insights into Operations Center fatigue and endurance.

My longtime friend and fifty-plus-year Coast Guard employee Mr. Ed Brady for his invaluable insights and telecommunications acumen in helping shape the technology chapter.

Mr. Arne Carr, Mr. John Fish, Mr. Dave Gallo and Mr. Vic Mastone for their help in developing the authors' understanding of underwater archaeology and deep-water wreck diving.

Charlie Mitchell, tug *Jaguar*, for his friendship and many contacts in the marine industry.

Acknowledgements

Mike DeConinck, Hokey's fellow fisherman and friend, for his stories and insights.

Mr. Don Lynch, Cuttyhunk, for his insights as a Sea Tow operator on the night of the *Sol e Mar* distress call and the week following.

1
"HOKEY" AND BILLY

Final preparations for the father-son team of William "Hokey" Hokanson and Billy Hokanson before their March 1990 fishing trip off Martha's Vineyard were routine. Little did they know this voyage would be their last and would end in disaster.

On March 21, 1990, the day before they left the Fairhaven, Massachusetts house they shared with Billy's uncle Ray and aunt Joyce Oliveira, they were outside with their two Rottweilers, Max and Snoopy. As usual, they could be found in the garage area working and puttering about, ensuring they were ready to leave the next day for Boston's Pier 7 and their fishing vessel, the *Sol e Mar* ("Sun and Sea" in Portuguese).

Joyce Oliveira recalls her nephew being excited about the trip, slipping off and leaving his favorite pair of sneakers on her back porch and heading out to mend *Sol e Mar*'s nets. She had no idea those sneakers would be the last tangible connection she and her husband, Ray, would ever have to Billy.

Ray later wrote, "As I leaned back on my workbench and had a cold one, I watched and listened as my wife talked to my nephew. She spoke to him in a soft and tender voice, touched his face to make him smile. She started to go back into the house, and with the embrace of a loved one, a silence filled the air. She started to walk away, and with a gentle smile she looked back and said, 'Have a safe trip.'"

Ray recalls the net was almost mended, and they "sat and talked about everything and nothing at all; my time with these fishermen had run aground.

As they left, I tried to hold on to one last look, but it was like trying to hold on to the tides."

Ray remembers wishing the fishermen a final farewell. The hour was late, and when Ray questioned Hokey about the odd departure timing, Hokey responded, "We go with the tide."

There would be no outward signs that something horrible would go wrong and cause the *Sol e Mar* to sink swiftly on the night of March 25, 1990. The demise of the vessel would be so fast, in fact, that Billy would barely have enough time to transmit an unclear, four-second radio distress call. Billy's distress call would be followed by a prank call that would set off a chain of errors by Coast Guard rescuers that would seal Hokey's and Billy's fates forever.

In commitment to their young nephew, Joyce and Ray have kept Billy's shoes outside their kitchen since the accident twenty-four years ago. They represent a memorial to him to this day. Joyce doesn't let anybody touch or move them. "We just shovel around them," she said.

The next day, on the drive to Boston's Pier 7, the family stopped at the Lobster Bowl restaurant in Wareham, Massachusetts, where Billy consumed

Billy Hokanson's weathered sneakers at Aunt Joyce and Uncle Ray's house. *Authors' collection.*

seven pieces of prime rib. People nearby must have been astonished at the tall (six-foot-two), handsome and lanky brown-eyed young man's ability to eat enough food to have satisfied a much heavier football player.

When his mother's husband, Eddie Ouellette, commented on the amount of food Billy had eaten, Billy eerily responded, "You have to live for today because tomorrow you don't know."

Throughout their short lives and even after their deaths, Hokey and Billy were different—spiritual and possessors of a thirst for life that defined them uniquely. To most everybody who knew him, "Hokey" Hokanson was a "happy-go-lucky guy," according to brother-in-law Ray Oliveira. Father and son looked as different as night and day. At five feet, six inches tall, Hokey was slightly pear shaped, with a round face, sparkly blue eyes and a unique, high-pitched voice that sounded unlikely to come from a rough-and-tumble New England fisherman.

But those who knew him understood that underneath Hokey's playful exterior and near constant smile was a rugged, hardy and driven individual. "He played hard and worked hard," Oliveira noted. Ray couldn't believe how Hokey could forge through pain when he had worked for a local paving

Hokey Hokanson reflecting after a hard day of fishing. *Image courtesy of Ellen (Hokanson) Ouellette.*

Hokey cleaning fish on the deck of *Sol e Mar*. *Image courtesy of Jeannie Berberian.*

company: "He'd come home with these blisters on his feet from the hot tar and put a purple salve on his feet and get right out there the next day."

Fellow fisherman Dave Dutra knew Hokey's endurance extended beyond his work on land. According to Dutra, "Hokey was known to fish continuously for days and remain awake just with coffee, his will and determination. No drugs. Hokey had more fishing time by hours than any other fisherman at the time."

Hokey was also a very giving person, sometimes even beyond his means. When he worked for a tire retreading company, he helped Ray create his own tire retread route. He was a generous man, according to Oliveira. "When [Ray's daughter] Becky wanted to go into a Miss Teen USA contest and needed expensive gowns and other items, Hokey said, 'What do you need?'" Fellow fisherman Dave Butcher was also a beneficiary of Hokey's giving ways, but in a different circumstance—as a competitor in his livelihood. When Butcher started to fish in 1986, Hokanson didn't hesitate to step forward to show him the ropes. According to Butcher, "When I first started dragging, Hokey showed me how to drag around Boston Harbor, which is a difficult place to fish," he added. Some people knew Hokey was way more generous than he could afford to be. Apparently, his mother, Sallie Hokanson, had helped him with his taxes and caused him to be in hot water with the IRS. Hokey shrugged off his mother's age-related mistakes and indicated he'd just have to work a little bit harder to catch up.

Hokey was also a "car nut." "He would bring home a different car at least once a month; he would fix them up and give them to people that didn't have a vehicle for some reason or another—he was very generous," said his ex-wife, Ellen (Hokanson) Ouellette.

Later in his life, Hokey abandoned all land-related work and chose a full-time life at sea. Ray Oliveira noted, "When they came in from a trip, they did what they needed to get the boat ready for the next trip." All bets were off when the fishing was done, and the fun began. Joyce Oliveira commented, "Hokey went out of his way to make sure everybody had a great time at his place. He built everybody a volleyball net and kept the party going and would just sit back and enjoy the festivities. Hokey loved his fish fries: calamari, lobster, scallops and yellow tail." Those fish fries and other parties were part of some of the best years at Hokey's Carver, Massachusetts home that he

Max, Hokey's beloved Rottweiler, stands security watch on *Sol e Mar*. *Image courtesy of Ellen (Hokanson) Ouellette.*

and ex-wife Ellen (Hokanson) Ouellette shared for the first ten years of their twenty-year marriage. But Hokey's interests were wide and diverse. According to Ellen, "Hokey loved animals. He was always bringing something home." Those who knew him understood he wanted to try his hand at farming, even though he had many other things going on in his life.

Hokey brought home a Shetland pony for his son when Billy was six years old. The pony didn't like to be ridden, and Billy was petrified of him. "All Billy did was cry," said Ellen. Next thing Ellen knew, Hokey "saw a bull in a field and asked the owner if he was for sale. Now we have a bull, and then [he got] a huge Morgan horse for me." But of course, Hokey never rode the horse, and Ellen had to break it in. "He just liked having animals," Ellen recounted. Another time, Ellen told of how Hokey "told Billy to sit on the sofa and close his eyes because he had a surprise for him. [Hokey placed] a small box carefully on Billy's lap, [and Billy] opened it. And out came fifty baby chicks that immediately scattered all over the living room—needless to say, they had to stay in Billy's room in a box because they were too small to be outside. Hokey was a character for sure. And you know who had to take care of all these animals, don't you?" But the farm idea and the home in Carver eventually gave way to a dedicated life of fishing and a move back to Fairhaven.

Hokey's yearly fishing routine, according to friend and *Sol e Mar* crewman Francis "Franny" Davis, "started out near Plymouth in the fall." After that, they "worked [their] way up to Boston for the New Year. In those days, [fishing] inside two miles [of shore] was closed for most of the year and opened January 1. We would be there at the stroke of midnight to drop the net and fish in areas closed most of the year. Saw the Boston fireworks from afar many years."

Billy's cousin Randy Oliveira, who also crewed on the *Sol e Mar*, recalled that "in the spring, Hokey would fish off Nomans Island and move and fish off Nantucket in the summer." Randy had been scheduled to be on the boat for that last March 1990 trip, but he "got a six-month plumbing job—that saved my life." Oliveira still regrets not having gone with Hokey and Billy on their last trip—"maybe I could have done something to help."

Hokanson, like many other fishermen, loved and collected guns. Franny Davis recalls:

> *One winter, we all got guns for Christmas presents, and we decided to bring them on the boat to test 'em out. Hokey had a new shotgun, black powder rifle and a handgun. I had my shotgun and a black powder rifle, a gift from*

The Sol e Mar Tragedy off Martha's Vineyard

Hokey Hokanson playing with codfish. *Image courtesy of Cheryl Best.*

> *Hokey. Billy had a couple of handguns, an AK47 knockoff and a black powder rifle. We got boarded by the Coast Guard on a routine check, and after all the licenses and permits were checked, the Coast Guard guy asks if we* [had] *any weapons on board. We proceed*[ed] *to lay out all said instruments of destruction on the bunk, and the Coast Guard chap says, "Jesus, you're better armed than we are." Then he asks, "Are they loaded?" to which Hokey responds in his rather high-pitched voice, "They don't work if they ain't loaded!"*

One time, when crewman Randy Oliveira had been working on the *Sol e Mar* for an extended period of time, he lost quite a bit of weight; he was extremely hungry and tired of eating Dinty Moore beef stew, which they always heated up over a Sterno can. Another boat offered to bring over a turkey dinner with all the fixings to Hokey and his crew. When the other boat passed the dinners to Randy on *Sol e Mar*, he immediately began to gorge himself on the food on the forecastle, ignoring his other shipmates. Hokey, seeing that Randy was piggishly consuming the food, "shot me in the ass with a gun using wadding," Randy said. Then the food was quickly shared.

Hokey had a serious side when it came to his weapons and the price of fish. One time, fellow fisherman Dave Dutra brought his fish to New Bedford by truck, and Hokey was offloading a load of sand dabs, a common flatfish, from the *Sol e Mar*. According to Dutra, "Hokey was 'negotiating' with the buyer to get one dollar a pound for sand dabs. The buyer told Hokey, 'You're not f——g getting one dollar a pound for sand dabs.'"

Hokey had been awake for three days, and his eyes were all bloodshot. The discussion with the buyer got heated, and Dutra saw Hokey reach into *Sol e Mar*'s pilothouse and pull out his pistol. Hokey then put two rounds into the buyer's building. Dutra recalls Hokey remarking, "I told you I'd get a dollar for dabs!"

Back in Hokey's early days of fishing, he and fellow fisherman Mike DeConinck were non-union fishermen during a union strike and had to be transported to an alternate fish auction in the buyers' armored car. When Hokey and Mike left the auction, there was no armored car, so they had to try to cross the picket line of angry fishermen. The mad fishermen began to kick Mike and Hokey and hurt their legs badly. When things started to get out of hand, Hokey brandished his silver-plated .44 Magnum, and the "seas parted," according to DeConinck. Both fishermen got out of there pronto in a Cadillac driven by Mike's wife at the time, Helen.

Hokey was all in when it came to his own education, especially when he was on the *Sol e Mar* at sea. Ray Oliveira said Hokey read "books galore, and many magazines from *Playboy* to Plato, he didn't do anything halfway. He could always win the who's who and what's what trivia contests." Billy's friend Saul Raposo was also impressed with Hokey's knowledge: "He was the first man outside my own father that made an impression on me growing up. He had so much knowledge. Hokey Sr. was always reading something. He always had something to read in the wheelhouse."

But the hard life of fishing, time away from home and commitment to various pursuits had a cost for Hokey in terms of his ability to support some family members. Hokey had a daughter, Cheryl Best, from his first marriage. Hokey and Best's mother had divorced when Cheryl was a couple years old. The decision was made not to tell Cheryl that Hokey was her real father. Best grew up in several different households, and Cheryl's mother's new husband adopted Cheryl when she was four years old. Cheryl didn't find out that Hokey was her father until she was about twelve.

Cheryl was shy as a young child. "I always felt insecure around other people," she said. "My mother and I were driving home from my dance class, and it was raining out and I asked her, 'Why do I have to go to my grandmother's house every weekend and my brother Scott doesn't have to go?' My mother told me that one of my nana's son's was my biological father. When we got home, my mother told her husband that she had told me about being Hokey's daughter, and they never discussed it again and wouldn't let me ask questions," Best said. "This caused much confusion in my life, and I turned to drugs and alcohol while in junior high school."

Cheryl wrote Hokey a letter when she was told he was her real father, and he answered. According to Best, "He just explained that he thought he was doing what was best."

Hokey's letter, according to Best, "was five pages long, with the last page being on navigation chart plotter paper because it was all he had. In the last line, he told me to listen to Lynyrd Skynyrd's song 'Freebird' because he felt that was the song of his life or being."

It would take many years, time away from her Fairhaven childhood neighborhoods and quiet reflection on Martha's Vineyard for Cheryl to resolve her inner turmoil. There was no such turbulence for her well-grounded brother, Billy.

One of Billy Hokanson's nicknames growing up was "Momma-hugger," according to his cousin Randy Oliveira. Billy and his mother, Ellen (Hokanson) Ouellette, had a very close relationship. According to Ellen, "When we were home watching television, Billy would always sit on the floor up against the sofa right next to my legs. He had the whole living room, but he always sat next to me. I still laid out his clothes and cut his meat at dinner, until he graduated from high school." Mother and son spent a lot of time together, especially when Billy's father was fishing alone or with others.

When Billy would go out for fun with friends, he'd often

Billy and his mother, Ellen, at his graduation in 1989. *Image courtesy of Eddie Ouellette.*

include his mother. According to Ellen, "When he went dirt bike riding with his friends, he always made sure I was there, taking pictures of them. I [still] have a large picture of him in midair on the wall in his room. We would go out for pizza, to a local pizza joint, play pool; he was such a good boy." Billy had other positive influences in his life besides his mother.

Cousin Randy and Billy lived in the same house for several years beginning when Billy was seven and Randy was nine. Randy took care of Billy like an older brother.

Both attended nearby New Bedford Vocational Technical High School, where Billy's nickname, according to friends, was "Poindexter." "He was smart as a whip, despite staying behind a year in fourth grade. He got all A's, and his teachers loved and respected him," Ouellette said.

Billy was extremely intelligent. He could look at a map with fifty state capitals and absorb the materials in a fraction of the time it took other people. According to his mother, "Billy loved to take things apart. One day, he had disassembled the transistor radio because, [he said,] 'I want to know how it works!'" And he was able to put it back together and have it function, too.

Eddie Ouellette spoke of how he had the *Hokey II* (Billy's boat) reengineered after Billy's death. Eddie had someone make several modern updates that all ended up being put back the "way Billy had them." None of the improvements, according to Eddie, "worked as well as Billy's original designs. Billy was naturally gifted."

Early on, Randy Oliveira was Billy's protector. One day, when Billy was at the Fairhaven skate rink, a kid stole his leather jacket. Billy called the elder Randy, who came right down and told the kids they could deal with him. Randy got Billy's jacket back. Along the way, Billy changed and became more self-confident and less self-focused. For example, his father, Hokey, bought Billy a new Arnold Schwarzenegger power lifting and body building book as a gift. Billy and Randy were using the book until Billy got mad at Randy and took the book and hid it. Sometime later, during a hockey game, Billy got whacked from behind by a dirty New Bedford hockey player. Even though the referee assessed a penalty to the miscreant player, Randy whacked the dirty player "right on his ass." A short time later, Randy found the Schwarzenegger book on his desk.

Despite his early self-focus and his mother's well-meaning and overly caring ways, Billy eventually began to mature in high school.

Randy also told the story about how Billy was unhappy that girls got to wear cooler clothing during the hot weather. The boys had to wear trousers year-round. As a form of protest, according to Randy, "Billy wore a black

Billy Hokanson a few weeks after getting his head shaved. *Image courtesy of Ellen (Hokanson) Ouellette.*

miniskirt and sneakers to school at our vocational school. Billy got into a lot of trouble for this, but the school changed its policy as a result."

Billy's boyhood defiance and assertions extended into other areas. Billy's aunt Joyce Oliveira recalls that "Billy and my son, Ricky, shaved their heads completely bald just before their high school senior pictures." The pictures were rescheduled. Joyce also recalled an occasion when Billy and some other hockey players shaved "crossed-sticks and their jersey numbers in their hair for a game." When their coach told them not to take off their helmets, Billy brazenly showcased his new hairdo for all to see.

Billy's changes were more than physical and emotional. Friend Saul Raposo had the same classes with Billy at Vocational Technical School—they studied and played Nintendo together. And according to Saul, "Billy would give you the shirt off his back." Saul also witnessed a different side of his friend Billy. "He was fearless with women, cars and the ocean. He was extremely loyal. Billy fought a bigger kid, who always picked on me, in the school parking lot, and I never forgot that." Saul also fished on *Sol e Mar* with Hokey and Billy. Saul recalls that "I almost died one time underway when we were in rough seas. I had my butt up against the stern A-frame, and the boat suddenly stopped when a giant wave came over the pilothouse and hit me square in the chest." Saul would have gone right out the stern chute if his waders hadn't got caught on the boat. According to Saul, "Billy was fearless and pulled him back aboard."

Saul knew that Billy was "proud of his Viking heritage." To this day, Saul still wears a key chain with a Viking icon on it that had been given to him by Billy's mother.

Billy liked flashy cars and pretty girls. After he became distracted trying to impress a girl, he crashed a newly acquired '69 Corvette Stingray. Billy's driving privileges were taken away by his mother.

Billy Hokanson after being tossed in Menemsha Harbor, Martha's Vineyard, on his sixteenth birthday. *Image courtesy of Ellen (Hokanson) Ouellette.*

So Billy tried another method. He wanted to go to McDonald's and pressured his mother's husband, Eddie Ouellette, for the keys to a different car. Eddie said, "Don't put me in that position." Clever Billy took Max, the Rottweiler, on a leash and had the dog tow him on his skateboard to McDonald's and through the drive-through! The girls were impressed, even without the Corvette.

Hokey's love life was no less interesting and unique. With two failed marriages in his past, he connected with his colorful redheaded neighbor, Jeannie Berberian, who reported, "I was coming off a failed and difficult marriage."

Hokey, according to Berberian, affectionately referred to her as "Bimbo." At one point, young Billy challenged his father's nickname for Berberian and told her, "Jeannie, you shouldn't let my father call you that; it's not very nice." To which Berberian responded, "It doesn't matter—your father knows I'm far from a bimbo. It's OK really."

But Jeannie and Hokey were a match from the start. According to Berberian, "Growing up, I was a tom boy, farm person, milked cows, shoveled shit and did physical labor." Berberian was convinced that her affinity for physical labor and willingness to get her hands dirty "attracted Hokey to me because I could get right on the boat and start working."

"I knew Hokey for nine to ten months before he died," Jeannie said. "I fell in love with him. Since I was ten years younger than Hokey, I used to address him as Mr. Hokanson," she noted. Berberian apparently saw what so many other people had seen. "He was a wonderful, happy, good-hearted person and a delight. I will never trade my time with Hokey," Berberian said.

One time, Billy gave Jeannie a baseball bat to take with her for protection when she walked to and from the *Sol e Mar*. Berberian said, "I will always love Billy for caring." Billy's protective ways extended to his mother as well. When Billy saw a sparkling engagement ring on his mother's hand, he said, "I am happy for you." But according to his mother, "Billy was perplexed that [my] husband-to-be, Eddie, hadn't asked him for his mom's hand in marriage."

Billy also routinely told Hokey's new girlfriends: "Don't get too serious—my dad's getting back together with my mom." He also "would get so mad if his father raised his voice to me, or spoke harshly to me," his mother said. But there was always a lighter side to Hokey's personality with family and friends alike.

In the aggregate, Billy was a handsome, talented young man who in several ways had eclipsed his father and surely would have gone on to bigger and better

things in life. To many who knew him, Billy had already learned and applied key values and skills that some people would never learn no matter how long they lived.

Hokey was a prankster and enjoyed teasing his friends and fellow mariners with great regularity.

Mike DeConinck from the fishing vessel *Millpoint* used to fish "side by side" with Hokey and the fishing vessel *Sol e Mar*. They started out as "greenhorns" back in the 1980s but found themselves in the minority among fishermen with their cutting-edge investments in the latest nets and electronically controlled drums. They became known for their success among the fleet of fishermen, who would often try to find their fishing spots. Mike and Hokey would spoof the other

Top: Hokey Hokanson and Jeannie Berberian on *Sol e Mar*. *Image courtesy of Cheryl Rasmussen.*

Left: Jeannie and Hokey at a high school reunion. *Image courtesy of Jeannie Berberian.*

The Sol e Mar Tragedy off Martha's Vineyard

Hokey Hokanson having fun. *Image courtesy of Cheryl Best.*

fishermen with bogus radio conversations that would have the other fishermen racing to other locations. It "drove them crazy," according to DeConinck.

Good friend Dave Butcher, captain of the fishing vessel *Resolute*, worked alongside Hokanson. "At the end of the day I would leave tools around the boat (I was at Fairhaven Shipyard). I'd leave fiberglass matt, tools and resin lying around. The next day when I went back to the boat, I'm told Hokey would put my gear in the fish hold so I could not find it, as a joke." On another occasion, Butcher attempted to get in his fish hold and found "about fifty brand-new fish totes that belonged to another boat!"

The Sol e Mar Tragedy Off Martha's Vineyard

One of the Hokansons' favorite places was Martha's Vineyard, Massachusetts. In 1974, the Vineyard was heavily featured in the bright limelight with the filming of the frightening movie *Jaws* in the fishing village of Menemsha and the town of Chilmark.

But for all its bright sunshine, the Vineyard harbored dark secrets. They include the iconic scandal where Mary Jo Kopechne died in a car accident at Chappaquiddick Island on July 18, 1969, as a passenger in a car driven by U.S. senator Edward M. "Ted" Kennedy. Senator Kennedy was accused of swimming off and not notifying officials until the following morning.

It was also an area where the Coast Guard's storied past took a turn for the worse on the night of November 23, 1970, when the crew of the Coast Guard cutter *Vigilant* returned defecting Latvian sailor Simas Kadurka to the trawler *Litva* just off Menemsha Bight. Kadurka's circumstance and the Coast Guard's inept handling of his asylum request were later featured in a book, *Day of Shame*, by Algis Ruksenas. But for all its past secrets, Martha's Vineyard, especially Menemsha Harbor, was always one of the Hokansons' favorite places. In another instance of comic relief, Hokanson and Butcher had both their boats tied up at Menemsha and had had a few beers. When Hokanson went ashore to run an errand, Butcher climbed *Sol e Mar*'s mast and "tied a small line from the top of its mast to the dock." So when the *Sol e Mar* got underway the next day and began to pull away, it caused the vessel to tip severely on its side due to the leverage from the line being tied to the dock.

Hokanson "never got mad," according to Butcher, but he always "got even." With Butcher's boat tied up after the latest Menemsha incident at a nearby shipyard for four days, it was open season for Hokanson. Four days later, Butcher found "a scallop dredge and a 250-pound fuel oil tank in his rigging." According to Butcher, "I never figured out how Hokanson got all that stuff up in my rigging."

Sometimes, Hokey and Billy pranked each other. According to Randy Oliveira, who periodically fished with the Hokansons on *Sol e Mar*, "Billy and Hokey were always joking on the boat. One time when the *Sol e Mar* was in Vineyard Haven, Billy and Randy had set up the winch such that Billy could swing out over the water. Hokey came back to the boat while this was going on, and Billy was fully dressed suspended out on the rope. Hokey released the line, and Billy got dunked after he tried unsuccessfully to shinny up the rope. Billy, drenched by the water, ran and jumped in Hokey's bunk, soaking the bedding."

For all Hokey's experiences, his awkward relationships with some women and his incredible depth of knowledge in many areas garnered from reading

Coast Guard Station Menemsha, Martha's Vineyard. *Image courtesy of U.S. Coast Guard.*

Hokey horsing around. *Image courtesy of Jeannie Berberian.*

on solitary fishing trips, he was mostly a simple, giving man driven to work hard and play hard in a complex world. While his son, Billy, lived only nineteen short years, many who knew him were envious of his strength of character, thirst for life and uncanny engineering abilities well beyond his age. Sadly, in a bitter twist of irony, a prankster would cause Billy and Hokey's death on the night of March 25, 1990. Eighty seconds after Billy issued his short, difficult-to-hear distress call, a hoax caller would say, "SOS, I'm sinking," followed by laughter. As a result, no boats or helicopters would be launched to save the day, several families would be torn apart and the fishing community of Fairhaven, Massachusetts, would never be the same.

2

DOMESTIC TERRORISM

Anatomy of Hoax Callers

The sleek red-and-yellow Air Med helicopter, piloted by former Coast Guard pilot John "Sean" Rafter, forty-nine, plunged into the frigid Casco Bay, Maine waters about 8:30 p.m. on the night of November 19, 1993. Unexpected head winds had caused the chopper to run out of fuel, dooming a burn victim patient, a flight nurse and a paramedic on board.

Paramedic Matthew T. Jeton, twenty-eight, of Portland; Nurse Donald M. McIntyre, fifty, of Manchester, New Hampshire; and burn patient Douglas Fernald, seventy, of East Sullivan, Maine, died in the crash. Fernald was burned on more than 30 percent of his body from burning leaves and was being transported to Maine Medical Center.

Rescuers from the Cape Elizabeth, Maine Water Extrication Team (WET), assisting the local Coast Guard, would save pilot Rafter after five hours of searching. Rafter told the *Boston Globe* a few days after the crash that he had become disoriented as the helicopter had flipped over, filled with water and sunk in eighty-five feet of water. Despite making two attempts to save his crew and passenger, only the pilot would survive after the pontoons snapped off the helicopter, providing Rafter a buoyant platform to paddle to a nearby island. The trek to the island would take two hours. Here, Rafter huddled behind a rock for three hours to stave off the chilling cold wind and hypothermia until he was spotted by rescuers.

The Coast Guard had dispatched a 110-foot cutter, a 41-foot utility boat and a helicopter to search for the downed aircraft. In addition to the WET team, the Coast Guard was being assisted by vessels from the Maine Marine

The Sol e Mar Tragedy Off Martha's Vineyard

Patrol, the Portland and Long Island fire departments and a commercial ferry, the *Island Holiday*.

Lieutenant Jerry Green, from Coast Guard Group Portland, said, "Conditions were rainy, with four- to six-foot swells and occasional eight-foot waves. The rains are going to hamper the search, but cloud cover helps because it prevents the moon from reflecting off the water surface." Rescuers liken the difficulty of finding a person in the water to spotting a basketball on the surface of the water. With cloud cover, the chances of locating the person were better because the moonlight wouldn't create a difficult, shiny background that would obscure a person's head.

The response from the public was overwhelming, with many mariners bringing their boats "out of mothballs" just to help with the search. Despite the freezing temperatures and blizzard conditions, more than twenty volunteer vessels, or "Good Sam's" in Coast Guard lexicon, would participate in the search for Rafter, his crew and the patient. But the very visible and chaotic circumstances would also attract another type of responder.

Unfortunately, the rescue was complicated further by the cowardly radio calls of a hoax caller on channel 16 VHF-FM, the primary distress coordination frequency. The Coast Guard's technology at the time would reveal only two critical facts. The hoax caller was on land, calling from the Portland side of Casco Bay, and he was mobile, probably using a handheld VHF-FM radio from a vehicle. The misleading calls misdirected search efforts, endangered rescuers unnecessarily, prolonged the search and sealed the fate of the missing people from the downed helicopter.

When a Good Sam vessel would make a radio report during the rescue, the hoax caller would clone the name of the real caller and deliberately misdirect rescuers in the wrong direction. The resulting dialogue went something like this:

(Good Sam) "Coast Guard Group Portland, I am reporting debris in the vicinity of Cushing Island, over."
(Group Portland) "Good Sam, this is Group. Are you in the vicinity of channel buoy number 3 over?"
(Hoax Caller) Group Portland, negative, I am right near channel buoy 17 over.
(Good Sam) Group Portland, we have someone playing with the radio; I am in position (radio screeches as the hoax caller keys his microphone at the same time).

THE SOL E MAR TRAGEDY OFF MARTHA'S VINEYARD

Because the prankster was transmitting at the same time as rescuers, a phenomenon called "stepping on a transmission," multiple additional calls were precipitated, delaying coordination as the crash victims' lives were sucked away by the forty-four-degree Atlantic waters.

Cape Elizabeth WET team member Joe Mokry recalled, "The hoax caller tried to direct responders toward the inner part of Casco Bay. We had our search orders outside Casco Bay in the area of Vaill Rock, and we were 'mission-focused' and ignored the extra noise. We finished our designated area [outside Casco Bay] and eventually found pilot Sean Rafter."

Mokry commented that "at the time of the WET team's deployment, there was great uncertainty of the location of the Air Med helicopter." He went on to indicate that "after several hours of searching, the WET had some decisions to make." Aware of the ongoing radio jousting with the hoax caller and faced with a need for a crew change out due to cold weather and exhaustion, the WET chose to maintain discipline and focus on its assigned search area. The WET's persistence paid off as one of its search vessels started to "run across bandages and other medical items," according to Mokry. Eventually, the WET discovered the broken sponsons that Air Med pilot Rafter had used to paddle to Vaill Island and rescued him.

In the after-event lessons learned session, WET members reasoned: "Large-area searches involving multiple assets, many untrained, are easier for the hoax caller to infiltrate as radio traffic is already heavy and many of the searchers freely communicate on working channels even when unnecessary." And the bottom-line lesson the WET learned, according to Mokry: "Cold, wet and tired searchers greet the hoax call with a certain amount of welcome as it appears to offer a quick solution to the search."

Despite the existence of the 1990 Studds Act, a federal law with severe criminal penalties for hoax callers, at the time of the Air Med crash in 1993, almost one-third of distress calls to the Coast Guard were thought to be hoax calls. There were so many calls, in fact, that the First Coast Guard District in Boston, responsible for the ocean area from Canada to Toms River, New Jersey, had formally established a Hoax Enforcement Action Team (HEAT).

The HEAT was an eclectic grouping of Coast Guard and maritime operators and law enforcement professionals from the local, state and federal agencies, as well as the Federal Communications Commission (FCC) and sometimes even psychiatric professionals. The FCC has the capability to triangulate radio hoax radio calls made from land. Traveling in special vans equipped with sensitive direction-finding equipment, FCC personnel could, under the right circumstances, drive up to a perpetrator's door and earmark the location for possible law enforcement action. The FCC's tracking capability based out of Boston would not be available until the day after the Air Med crash.

Within a few days after Rafter's rescue, the enforcement team convened a meeting at the Group Portland offices to collectively review the audiotapes from the night of the crash. The room was jammed with pissed-off people upset that someone would willfully disrupt their rescue attempts. Local fishermen, who had volunteered to search, knew better than anyone in the room the consequences of delaying searchers in harsh conditions. Many knew other fishermen who had been immersed in cold water and understood the chances of survival were slim, even under the best of circumstances.

The LEOs, or law enforcement officers, all knew the lost Air Med emergency personnel. They had responded to the same rescue calls and had formed tight bonds, similar to military units in war. Sometimes, emergency medical service (EMS) personnel patched up and bandaged law enforcement when they were injured or wounded while making arrests. The LEOs and EMSes had one another's backs—a long-valued tradition. They were brothers and sisters united in a common cause of public safety.

The radio audiotape was initially played to see if anybody recognized the hoaxster's voice. Nobody had a solid sense of who the caller was until the tape was replayed a few more times. This time, the local psychologist, Peter Smith, from Southern Maine EMS spoke up and gave his assessment. "I don't know who this man is, but I can tell you about him." The room got very quiet. The hoax caller was in his "mid-to-late forties, [a] smoker, reasonably well educated, from the Midwest," Smith stated. The next pronouncement really drew the group's attention, animating the LEOs further as they scratched furiously on their notepads. "[There is a] strong possibility this might be a disabled person, who desires the inclusivity of being part of the search heroics and being able to control the action anonymously."

An explosion of dialogue on a potential hoaxster emerged, and several Portland LEOs thought they had an idea about a person of interest who fit the profile.

Subsequent to the HEAT discussion, LEOs sought out the person of interest but could never pin the hoax calls on this individual. The Coast Guard Group never received similar radio calls from this hoax caller, but they continue to receive many more false distress calls. Billy Hokanson's March 25, 1990 prankster was also never caught and remains at large.

So what is the standard profile for hoax callers? Most hoax callers haven't been caught, so thorough academic analysis has not been conducted.

Experienced rescuers, radio watch standers and the FCC believe a healthy percentage of hoax callers are youths, ages twelve to fifteen, amusing themselves with their parents' marine radios.

Psychologist Peter Smith, former clinical director of the Southern Maine EMS Critical Incident Stress Management team, commented on hoax callers' potential profiles. "While no firm diagnosis can be made from listening to a radio tape, these are definitely control-seeking individuals with characteristics of antisocial personality disorder [according to] DSM-V [*Diagnostic and Statistical Manual of Mental Disorders*, fifth edition], the newest mental health reference. This diagnosis [was] previously referenced as [a] psychopath [for which the] key element[s] [are] no conscience, reckless disregard for the safety of others [and] in fact, *pleasure* in seeing others suffer due to the caller's powerful influence, delighting in causing responders to be furious, etc."

Smith went on to theorize: "I think now (likely more than in the early '90s) what kids (of all ages—including some very immature adults) see in violent video games is also something that hoax callers might try to 'one-up.'"

Smith, whose duties in 1993 included the responsibility for providing psychological crisis response to first responders in southern Maine, including Coast Guard members, recalled the deep, chronic frustration that plagued rescuers because of the frequency of so many hoax callers. With the Portland case, Coast Guard communications personnel and others were psychologically debriefed because of the loss of their fellow responders in the helicopter crash and the added frustrations from the hoax caller.

Coast Guard responders and communications personnel were "trying to direct limited resources to specific places only to later learn that [they] were being misled, elevating stress right off the charts." In Smith's opinion, hoax callers "were early terrorists."

Despite the passage of time since the 9/11 terrorist attacks, there is no universally accepted definition of "terrorist." However, in general, one accepted definition indicates that "terrorists are those who perpetrate criminal acts in order to provoke a state of terror in the general public, a group of persons or particular persons for political purposes [that] are in any circumstance unjustifiable, whatever the considerations of a political, philosophical, ideological, racial, ethnic, religious or any other nature that may be invoked to justify them."

Operational procedures have been fine tuned over the last twenty-four years to minimize the chances that hoax callers will mislead rescuers like they did on the night of March 25, 1990. Radio equipment has been upgraded

The Sol e Mar Tragedy Off Martha's Vineyard

Sightings of Coast Guard cutters, like this one, patrolling New York Harbor became much more frequent after 9/11. *Image courtesy of U.S. Coast Guard.*

to link audio recordings with their corresponding archived radio lines of bearing, facilitating quick retrieval and review of protocols. Yet today's Coast Guard and other first responders still suffer from an unacceptable number of wasteful and dangerous hoax calls.

The hoax caller phenomenon is not only a Coast Guard national problem but also an international phenomenon among first responder organizations. Katherine Isoardi of Queensland Ambulance Service (QAS) in Brisbane, Queensland, Australia, noted that "Punjab province in Pakistan—apart from the startlingly large numbers of calls received per annum—almost 24 million calls over around 5.5 years—the exceedingly high overall rate (89.5%) of vexatious or malicious calls to this emergency system almost belies belief."

Author Isoardi remarked on systems in Australia: "The QAS Emergency Medical System is large by world standards, with in excess of 3,000 front line operational staff. For the 2008–2009 financial year, the QAS received 493,312 Triple Zero (their version of 9-1-1) emergency medical calls, of which 90.27% were answered within 10 seconds of presentation. A further 242,000 non-emergency calls were received by their emergency call centres. In excess of 8,000 cases were determined to be either hoax calls, or no patient was found at the scene by paramedics (representing less than 2% of the Triple Zero call presentations)." Author Isoardi indicated that the major difference between Pakistan and Australia's EMS call systems was Australia had previously invested heavily in an aggressive educational system after a tough anti-hoax law was passed. That effort was complemented with a new call triage system that prioritized legitimate calls for help.

According to Dr. Richard Lumb, a twenty-four-year police veteran and former project director of Public Safety and Corrections Research at the Center for Health Policy, Planning and Research at the University of New England, "This is a critical area that plagues police, fire and other first responders. Time and resources utilized in prank calls, or the disruption of services where someone was keying a mike and not allowing emergency services to communicate, is life-threatening. With all the sophistication in communications we would think this does not happen."

Unfortunately, with today's societal fixation on reality TV shows in which individuals hoax one another and social media, the opportunities to conduct prank calls in multiple communication mediums is readily available. A quick perusal of the Internet shows websites dedicated completely to effecting hoax calls of different varieties. On just one website, prankcall.com, users are given a choice of sixteen different hoax calls that can be perpetrated in three different languages. Callers can choose from the top-rated "You Kicked My Dog" to "She's Late," a pregnancy spoof. One could dismiss the phenomenon except for the fact that the prank user numbers range from fifty thousand to over half a million for each type of call.

According to Dr. Lumb, "When times are quiet and events like the Martha's Vineyard (*Sol e Mar*) occur, we can only imagine if a devastating event occurred and covered the entire eastern seaboard." Lumb believes the anatomy of a hoax caller's psychology "emerges from several psychological manifestations including a single or mix of the following potential motivations: boredom; anger; striking out, or a payback for something unrelated; the thrill of being able to do this, a quest for disruption because it is fun to cause confusion; someone who likes the potential of harm being done; and to pull something off and not get caught. For some criminals, like other challenges, it is getting away with it—to see if it can be done and do it!"

According to Lumb:

> *The most scary pranksters are the psychopaths, like the guys who sent biological toxic powders through the mail, this is another form of negative behavior to see if danger, chaos and death can be created. Deviance takes*

many forms, not the least of which is an attempt to extract power over others while not getting caught or harmed themselves. Their harmful manner is cowardly, for they have not the guts to step to the front and take a chance on getting away with it. The inner motivations are many and emerge as justification in the fulfillment of some hurt or anger or past harm (real or imagined). And then, when they are able to carry out their damage, they feel vindicated and/or justified.

Coast Guard personnel don't know if *Sol e Mar*'s hoax caller even heard Billy Hokanson's distress call or if he was just reacting to the Coast Guard's call outs attempting to respond to Hokanson. And they don't know if Billy heard the hoax caller's prank call. Ultimately, responders may never know which category of prankster wrought his particular form of perverse manipulation and terrorism on the night of March 25, 1990.

Was he a thrill-seeking teenager? Someone with a vendetta against the Coast Guard? A malicious psychopath determined to harm others? Or, as Dr. Smith suggests, a terrorist who knowingly strikes fear in a particular group of people? The results were the same regardless of the psychological motivations—Hokey and Billy Hokanson died cold, lonely and swift deaths.

3

"WE'RE SINKING, WE NEED HELP NOW!"

The skipper of the fifty-eight-foot dragger *Sol e Mar*, William "Hokey" Hokanson, was no stranger to the perils of the sea. His mother, Sallie, had gotten him and his other siblings from school in 1952, when he was just six years old, to wait at the Fort Phoenix overlook located in Fairhaven, Massachusetts, for their father's return from sea. However, Fritz Hokanson never came back from his fishing trip in the fishing vessel *Paolina*. He and five other *Paolina* crewmen are all thought to have perished in a horrific winter storm while returning from fishing near the *Nantucket* lightship on February 14, 1952.

Despite losing his father, Hokey Hokanson became a fisherman like his father was. Years after his father's death, Hokey and two of his brothers all somehow survived their own horrific storm on the ocean. All three brothers swore they would never return. But Hokey Hokanson did not heed nature's first warning and returned to the sea to continue fishing. New England fishermen sometimes work in the worst of weather, knowing the payoff at the dock with a load of freshly caught and iced fish can fetch sums of money that would takes weeks, if not months, to earn in conventional jobs. Coast Guard rescue personnel, some who are commercial fishermen themselves, know the fishermen's routine of re-provisioning, refueling, offloading and getting underway for work despite bad weather. The routine can sometimes cause complacency when it comes to recognizing risk. What would seem harrowing and risky to an ordinary landlubber becomes commonplace and "normal" through repetition to some mariners. A little more than thirty-

The Sol e Mar Tragedy off Martha's Vineyard

The *Nantucket* lightship (LS 112) as it heads offshore to its station, near where grandfather Fritz Hokanson's boat is believed to have sunk. *Image courtesy of U.S. Coast Guard.*

Coast Guard lightship *Nantucket* transiting to its assigned station. *Image courtesy of U.S. Coast Guard.*

eight years after the *Paolina*'s sinking and Fritz Hokanson's death on March 22, 1990, Hokey Hokanson and his son, Billy, set sail from Pier 7 in Boston, Massachusetts, in the *Sol e Mar*. They planned a five-day trip to catch

Billy and his girlfriend, Kerri Rasmussen, celebrate. *Image courtesy of Jeannie Berberian.*

flounder. Young Billy Hokanson contacted his girlfriend, Kerri Rasmussen, on the boat's cellular phone a few days later, about noon on Sunday, March 25. The two spoke normally but were continually interrupted by static and the calls dropping due to poor cellular reception. Nothing said during the phone call gave any indication of the nature of the tragedy that would occur later that same day. In fact, Billy reassured his girlfriend that he and his dad would return to port the evening of the following Tuesday, March 27, slightly earlier than their forecasted schedule since fishing had been good.

At about 8:30 p.m. on March 25, the fishing vessel *Resolute* and its skipper, Dave Butcher, met up with the *Sol e Mar* and gave them a paravane. Paravanes are "water kites" that effectively help guide trolling lines and keep them at a desired depth for the type of fishing that is being attempted. Like a kite, they can be adjusted higher or lower in the water column depending on the type of fish and bottom depth in the area. According to Butcher, "*Sol e Mar*'s outriggers were extended out and stowed in the up position." Butcher passed the paravane to Billy Hokanson, and Butcher told him: "If you need anything, just give me a holler." Billy responded, "We're good, thanks."

Again, nothing seemed amiss at the time the paravane was passed from the *Resolute* to the *Sol e Mar*, and Butcher sailed north toward Nomans Island to resume fishing. However, less than an hour later, at 9:18 p.m., young Billy Hokanson made an urgent, four-second call for help on VHF-FM channel 16 that was received by Coast Guard rescue stations at Brant Point on Nantucket, Menemsha on Martha's Vineyard and at the Group Woods Hole Operations Center, the regional rescue headquarters. The Coast Guard's Brant Point Nantucket station was the only station to have received a 240-degree radio direction finding (RDF) line of bearing indicating the direction of the *Sol e Mar*'s distress call from Nantucket. A line of bearing told the Brant Point Station that the *Sol e Mar*'s distress call had come from the general direction of Nomans Island. The Coast Guard's RDF, or radio direction finding accuracy at the time, according to Rear Admiral Rich Rybacki, First District commander, was unfortunately "plus or minus five degrees."

The call definitely piqued the concerns of some rescuers because of the panic in the caller's voice, but unfortunately, Billy Hokanson didn't or couldn't give *Sol e Mar*'s geographic position, and the name of the boat was either garbled or not clear to Coast Guard rescuers because of static on the radio. No nearby fishing vessels, required by maritime law to monitor the channel 16 VHF-FM distress channel, reacted to Hokanson's plea for help. Later analysis would reveal that a private land radio site did hear the *Sol e Mar*'s urgent call for help.

At the time of the *Sol e Mar*'s distress call, Mr. Don Lynch, longtime resident of Cuttyhunk Island and Sea Tow operator, heard portions of Billy's call. Sea Tow is one of several commercial at-sea salvage and tow operator services that have worked cooperatively alongside the Coast Guard, primarily during non-life-threatening circumstances, consistent with federal laws since September 1988.

In a 2013 interview, Lynch indicated that on the night of the sinking, at approximately 9:18 p.m., he believes he heard "MAYDAY, MAYDAY, I'm going, or" and nothing else. He recalled that he did not hear a name of a vessel, but what he did hear, according to Lynch, was "quick and loud and clear."

Mr. Lynch did not know it was *Sol e Mar* and indicated he would have recognized Hokey Hokanson's distinctive voice had Hokey made the distress call. Mr. Lynch hesitated to directly intervene as a commercial salvage operator in what was a serious Mayday call because "it was the Coast Guard's (vice Sea Tow's) business."

THE SOL E MAR TRAGEDY OFF MARTHA'S VINEYARD

An aerial view of Coast Guard Station Menemsha, Martha's Vineyard, in quieter times. *Image courtesy of U.S. Coast Guard.*

Coast Guard records indicate that Lynch did follow up with a call to nearby Menemsha Station nearly a week later, on April 1, 1990, at 1:40 p.m., after the vessel was reported overdue and the Coast Guard started its search for *Sol e Mar*. The Coast Guard's continual broadcasts caught his attention during a routine fueling of his boat in Menemsha. He recalls getting in touch with Coast Guard Station Menemsha to make sure they had also heard the call on March 25. And according to Lynch, "They had."

The Hokansons could not have known that the *Sol e Mar* was operating in a radio "dead zone," notorious for making radio communications difficult, even impossible. Unfortunately for the *Sol e Mar* crew, Coast Guard procedures and equipment (at some locations) did not yet require or allow radio watch standers to record every radio call and did not require watch standers to play back recorded tapes for questionable distress calls. What happened next, however, would seal the Hokansons' fate forever. Within one minute and twenty seconds of young Billy's distress call, another call—an obvious hoax—came in to the Group Woods Hole Operations Center. In a sarcastic

The Sol e Mar Tragedy off Martha's Vineyard

voice, the caller said, "SOS, I'm sinking," followed by laughter. The voice was not Billy Hokanson's voice. But the hoax caller's few words, without the checks and balances that would come from later Coast Guard procedures, began an uninterrupted error chain that destroyed any chance of the two Hokansons being rescued. Only the Group Woods Hole Operations Center heard the obvious hoax call, and no lines of bearing were received. An alert Coast Guard watch stander from Nantucket's Brant Point station then queried the Group Woods Hole command center about Billy Hokanson's distress call. But Woods Hole's radio watch stander thought he was asking about the obvious hoax call and dismissed the inquiry.

Three stations heard Billy Hokanson's 9:18 p.m. distress call, and Brant Point received a direction-finding line of bearing toward the *Sol e Mar*'s location. Later analysis would suggest the hoax caller was within the line of sight of the Group Woods Hole antenna and transmitting on low power, from either a boat or car. This explains why neither the Coast Guard Stations at Brant Point, Nantucket, nor those in Menemsha on Martha's Vineyard heard the hoax call. These dynamics beg critical questions. Why didn't the Group Woods Hole watch standers notice that they were the only site to receive the later obvious hoax call? And why wasn't the Brant Point direction-finding line of bearing pursued? Why wasn't a helicopter dispatched from the nearby Coast Guard Air Station on Cape Cod and flown down the line of bearing? Why wasn't the forty-four-foot motor lifeboat from Coast Guard Station Menemsha launched? It would take weeks and several investigations before answers and insights would shed light on these and other questions. The next day, Monday, *Resolute* skipper Butcher saw Billy's mother, Ellen Ouellette, at Kelly's Boat Yard in Fairhaven. She asked Butcher if he'd heard from her ex-husband, Hokey. Butcher said, "I saw him the day before."

Ouellette had tried repeatedly to contact the *Sol e Mar* after March 25 "without luck." Acquaintances and others assured her that her ex-husband and son were fine and probably just out of range and into some good fishing. But it was unlike Billy to not call every day.

After several days without contact, Mrs. Ouellette became panicky. On Friday night at about 9:30 p.m., March 30, about three days after the *Sol e Mar* was due to return to home port, the Coast Guard at Boston reacted to Mrs. Ouellette's report of the overdue vessel and initiated a massive rescue case involving multiple cutters and aircraft searching more than ten thousand square miles between Long Island Sound and Martha's Vineyard.

The search area was unusually large because Billy Hokanson's distress call and Brant Point's direction-finding bearing had not yet been linked to

The Sol e Mar Tragedy Off Martha's Vineyard

the case, and searchers theorized the *Sol e Mar* could have ranged a good distance since it last rendezvoused with the fishing vessel *Resolute* on the night of March 25 and its intended return to Fairhaven on March 28.

The Coast Guard's search effort included issuing an Urgent Marine Information Broadcast (UMIB) on the radio. UMIBs alert other mariners and the public in an attempt to involve them in helping rescuers determine the location of vessels reported missing or overdue. Radio traffic on channel 16 VHF-FM at the time was always congested with boaters—new and old, ignorant of radio procedures and lacking discipline—who used the distress frequency to check whether their radios were operational, misusing the emergency frequency and unnecessarily jamming the channel. Fishermen were just as bad, chattering about their fishing luck on their current trips or, worse, turning off the radio altogether so as not to be annoyed by the noise. About 10:00 p.m. on Sunday, April 1, 1990, a week after young Billy initiated his urgent plea for help, the Coast Guard suspended its search for the *Sol e Mar*. According to Ouellette, "The commanding officer called to inform me that the search was called off because a marine salvage company operator on Cuttyhunk Island called them when he heard what was going on and said he remembered hearing a Mayday call from a boat on Sunday, March 25, 1990, around 9:15 that sounded like the *Sol e Mar* or a Portuguese name. The Coast Guard Group in Woods Hole played back the tapes from that night and cleaned it up when they realized that they had heard it, too. But because of a second call, eighty seconds later, which sounded like a hoax, they took the first one as a hoax, too, and disregarded it."

With Cuttyhunk's Mr. Don Lynch's tip about the March 25 Mayday call, recordings of the radio transmission from the night of the sinking were recovered, cleaned up and enhanced. Billy Hokanson's call now clearly indicated: "This is the fishing vessel *Sol e Mar*. This is a Mayday. This is the fishing vessel *Sol e Mar*; we're sinking. We need help now!" On April 5, 1990, a Coast Guard helicopter on a law enforcement patrol found a red-orange fisherman's survival suit five miles south of Martha's Vineyard. The suit contained no definitive markings, but Hokanson family members viewed the suit the following day at the Coast Guard Air Station at Otis Air Base on Cape Cod and identified it as coming from the *Sol e Mar*. One of the Hokansons' dogs, either Max or Snoopy, was also reported to have washed ashore near Gay Head on Martha's Vineyard.

And so it was that the seafaring Hokanson family would descend into mourning as the Atlantic Ocean claimed two more members of their clan

A Coast Guard Sikorsky HH-52 involved in rescue training. *Image courtesy of U.S. Coast Guard.*

doing what they loved best: fishing. Now, the family members and friends demanded answers from the Coast Guard to difficult questions that would not come for months and, in some cases, years.

4
SOL E MAR INVESTIGATIONS

For the families involved, closure in sea tragedies takes a lot of time and is often facilitated by something tangible, like the recovery of a loved one's body. But in the *Sol e Mar* case, the sea did not give up the bodies of skipper William "Hokey" Hokanson or his son, Billy Hokanson, for their families and friends to mourn at ceremonies.

Sometimes, finding the sunken vessel, the last place family members were known to have lived or worked, gives solace to friends and loved ones. For maritime investigators, it can also give clues as to why tragedy struck in the first place. In late April 1990, Mike DeConinck, friend of Hokey Hokanson, led a crew of twelve volunteers aboard the borrowed contract vessel *Marlin* to search for the *Sol e Mar* off Nomans Island near Martha's Vineyard. *Marlin*'s trip had been financed by family friend Jeff Linberg, owner of Linberg Marine, Inc., of Fairhaven, Massachusetts. He had also been young Billy Hokanson's youth hockey coach since the time Billy was four. Linberg and other Hokanson friends had raised $18,000 to finance the trip to find the *Sol e Mar*.

Search efforts began in the vicinity of where *Sol e Mar* had rendezvoused with the fishing vessel *Resolute* on the night of the sinking. Dick Searles from Linberg Marine indicated:

A preliminary starting point for the search had been roughly calculated by myself as I was very familiar with wind and tidal currents—or in nautical terms, set and drift—and the sum of all information known, including time of last sighting based on range and bearing as shown on the fishing vessel

THE SOL E MAR TRAGEDY OFF MARTHA'S VINEYARD

The *Marlin* all-volunteer crew. *Front row, left to right*: unknown ROV pilot, Ron Archambault, diver Billy Avila; *back row, left to right*: diver Dave Bittner, unknown *Marlin* mate, Mike DeConinck, Joe Williams, *Marlin* captain/owner Ed Benedict, unknown side scan operator, diver John Bittner, unknown. *Image courtesy of Dick Searles.*

> Resolute's *radar, wind direction and velocity at time of last sighting and hypothetical tidal drift based on tide and geographical currents known for that area.*

Stopped and adrift, searchers did not exactly know where to begin. *Marlin* anchored out the night before work began because of a faulty remotely operated vehicle (ROV). The ROV carried a small camera capable of providing a glimpse into the murky depths 138 feet below.

Beth David, writer, editor and publisher of the *Fairhaven Neighborhood News* in 2006, entitled the section that described the hunt for the wreck "A Needle in a Haystack." Hokanson family friend Dick Searles remarked at "how difficult it is to find something out there. Especially on the ocean bottom, a vast unseen desert not visible to the naked eye, but only detected and analyzed by short-range side-scan sonar towed behind the search vessel and an experienced and trained operator." But suddenly, when they started work the next day, a harbor seal, far from its normal home environment, circled the boat a few times and seemed to say, according to Searles, "OK, you guys are here, so I can go now." The seal quickly left the area.

THE SOL E MAR TRAGEDY OFF MARTHA'S VINEYARD

The harbor seal, far from its normal environment, guides the *Marlin* crew to find the *Sol e Mar* in April 1990. *Image courtesy of Dick Searles.*

Beth David went on to explain that "folklore surrounding seals dates back hundreds of years and includes stories of seals shedding their skins to become human. Men steal and hide the skins of beautiful females to force them to live on land, but eventually they find their skins and return to the sea. Their connection to their human families, especially their children, remains forever." Searles promoted the sea's mysteries and said, "If you take any stock in the folklore of the sea, it is said they guard the spirit of people lost at sea. It was a really sobering experience."

Marlin's crew decided to search right where the seal directed them. A short time later, at 1:00 p.m. on Tuesday, April 24, 1990, side-scan sonar imagery revealed a target about fifty-five feet long sitting on the bottom. The position of the underwater wreck was not far from where *Sol e Mar* had last rendezvoused with the *Resolute*, forty-five minutes before Billy Hokanson's distress call.

When the underwater remotely operated vehicle equipped with a camera was lowered from the deck of the *Marlin*, DeConinck immediately recognized the top of the *Sol e Mar*'s wheelhouse on the first pass across the wreckage. Dick Searles noted:

> *The very first physical sign that presented itself on the ROV video screen aboard the* Marlin *was a steel cable, looking fresh and without a covering*

A diver on a platform prepares to be lowered down to the *Sol e Mar*. *Image courtesy of Dick Searles.*

of bottom sediment or marine growth, which was lying on the surface of the sandy bottom, not totally unusual—fishing vessels have been known to part their net towing cables that "hang up" on old wrecks. But soon after this sighting of the cable, a small red-and-green rubber hose was seen, and

The Sol e Mar Tragedy Off Martha's Vineyard

to the trained observer, this was the hose from an oxygen/acetylene cutting torch, standard equipment on all fishing vessels. This was unusual, so the ROV pilot followed the colored hose to see where it led. And as the ROV video camera followed, a snow-white fiberglass radar cover was passed, and soon the wheelhouse of a small dragger came into view, windows closed, resting in silence on the cold bottom. Constrained excitement was felt by all, floating above the Sol e Mar, *peacefully at anchor, high above the sunken wreck where we each, in our own way said a silent prayer.*

Focusing on the vessel's gallows frame, the words painted in white letters—*Sol e Mar*—were evident. Joe Williams, then yard manager of Linberg Marine in Fairhaven, Massachusetts, the main organizer for the trip, remarked, "The odds of that piece of metal landing face up and us finding it are incredible."

A Hang Up?

Most of the volunteers on the *Marlin* were convinced that the *Sol e Mar*, now resting on its side under 138 feet of water, had gotten hung up on one of two sunken wrecks that lay on the bottom in the area. The area near the sunken wrecks was a favorite hiding and feeding location for fish and likewise a favorite fishing spot for local draggers.

The *Marlin* volunteer crew believed the weather the night of the *Sol e Mar* sinking would have created a perfect set of circumstances that spelled the demise of the vessel. Weather reports from the night of the sinking indicated there were seven-foot seas driven by stiff twenty-knot southwesterly breezes and a thirty-eight-degree air temperature. These sea and weather conditions were such that skipper Hokanson would have put out his trawl net with a "following sea" coming from the stern of the vessel.

The *Marlin*'s volunteers suggested that if the *Sol e Mar*'s nets had hung up suddenly on one of the nearby wrecks, skipper Hokanson would have had mere seconds to react to slow the forward motion of the boat before the vessel's stern would have "squatted" down, allowing tons of cold North Atlantic water to rush in over the aft end of the boat.

Fellow fisherman Mike DeConinck and Hokey used to fish the area where the *Sol e Mar* sank, and both knew where the two sunken boats where nets could get hung up were located. Mike believes a possible contributing factor for the rapid sinking was that Hokey had trimmed the coaming (the frame) on *Sol e Mar*'s aft hatch from a height of twelve to fifteen inches down to about four to six inches high. Hokey did this for efficiency purposes, as he often fished single-handed. With a lower coaming height, things could be lifted in and out from below much easier. It could also allow flooding waters to enter the vessel faster than normal.

Franny Davis, Hokanson's friend and sometimes a crewmate on the *Sol e Mar*, suggested:

> *At the time, we had a scallop rig lashed to the starboard side of the boat that gave her a little list. Hokey had his "number-one son," Max, the Rottweiler, and they had just got*[ten] *a new Rot puppy, Snoopy. We blocked off the after scuppers so the pup*[s] *wouldn't get washed overboard. Of course, no one will know for sure, but I think the net might* [have] *got hung on the starboard side, sunk the rail and, with nowhere* [for the water] *to go out the scuppers, took on more water and capsized.*

But family members were skeptical of some of these theories. As far as whether or not the *Sol e Mar* had been fishing and hung up on another sunken fishing vessel, *Resolute* fisherman and skipper Dave Butcher said Billy was "back on the stern of the vessel mending nets at the time [about 8:30 p.m.] when I passed them a paravane." Ellen Ouellette inferred from Butcher's observations that it was highly doubtful that the *Sol e Mar* had even been fishing at the time of the 9:18 p.m. distress call. She implied that the theories that the *Sol e Mar* had hung up on another sunken fishing vessel while fishing were not possible because the *Sol e Mar*'s nets may not have been deployed at the time of the sinking. She also indicated that "the divers' underwater video shows *Sol e Mar*'s nets piled up on the sand near the stern of the vessel and no other vessels in the vicinity."

THE SUBMARINE THEORY

Years after the sinking, a trusted family friend advised Billy's mother that a "navy official had confessed to the friend that he had lived with the guilt that his submarine had sunk the *Sol e Mar*." Billy's uncle, Ray Oliveira, commented on the submarine theory and said that he'd had an experience when he was fishing for shark and tuna in the vicinity of Nomans Island when a sleek, silent U.S. Navy attack submarine approached them and directed them: "Do not deviate your course." Oliveira commented, "A sub fin could have caught the nets and drug *Sol e Mar* under quickly."

Oliveira's theory was somewhat supported by the wide debris field on the bottom seen on the *Marlin*'s ROV camera footage. But unfortunately, the underwater video suddenly ceased as the ROV approached the *Sol e Mar*. According to Ellen Ouellette, the *Marlin*'s "camera operator admitted he forgot to press the record button for some reason when the ROV approached the wreck."

Further adding to the mystery was the fact that the *Marlin* dive vessel had been shadowed by a navy surface unit while it had positioned near the wreck site on the night before the dive. According to Ellen Ouellette, "The navy vessel was watching *Marlin*'s activities the whole time but did not respond to *Marlin*'s radio calls at any time."

Coast Guard Conclusions

Coast Guard investigators in 1990 were less certain of any of these explanations and offered theories but no conclusions to solve the mystery. On July 10, 1990, almost seven months after the sinking, an investigative report from the Coast Guard's Marine Safety Office in Providence, Rhode Island, indicated the "the apparent cause of this casualty cannot be determined." Exploring the vessel's inspection records and discussing the tragedy with Mike DeConinck, a Hokanson family friend and owner of a sister vessel to *Sol e Mar*, Coast Guard investigators determined several possible contributory causes to the sinking.

Investigators determined that three years before the sinking, a new rudderpost was installed in *Sol e Mar* without a packing gland that is designed to seal the post and inhibit flooding. With a history of the rudderpost leaking, including a November 1989 incident where the vessel flooded through to the engine room deck and a second event in January 1990, investigators focused on this aspect of vessel safety when they considered the possibilities. Hokey Hokanson did not report any of these problems to the Coast Guard, as required.

Many New England fishing vessels at the time of the sinking were converted to multipurpose fishing vessels, allowing year-round fishing, since federal fisheries' regulations no longer allowed unrestricted fishing in any single fishery. Here, Coast Guard investigators keyed in on *Sol e Mar*'s conversion to a dragger capable of scalloping and the added weight in the area of the wheelhouse: "Additional weight, including a heavy dredge, boom and shucking house was added to the main deck causing a permanent 10 degree port list." Adding to the concerns was that skipper Hokanson had not bothered to verify the vessel's stability after these changes were made. An unstable vessel could have created added risk for capsizing suddenly without notice.

Providence, Rhode Island Coast Guard officers also theorized that on the day of the sinking, *Sol e Mar* was "operating without paravanes (birds) which increase vessel stability when in use." Forty-five minutes prior to young Billy Hokanson's distress call on March 25, 1990, the nearby fishing vessel *Resolute* had provided the *Sol e Mar* with one paravane. According to the Coast Guard, "Any attempt to deploy this paravane would have required the vessel's crew to raise the vessel's boom, thereby causing a reduction in the vessel's stability."

Also of concern was the fact that Hokanson routinely traveled with two of *Sol e Mar*'s freeing ports (openings on the side of the boat strategically placed to allow water to run overboard instead of remaining on deck) covered over to prevent the two pet dogs, Max and Snoopy, from being washed overboard. Investigators suggested the added weight and dynamic movement of any sloshing water on deck could also have contributed to the vessel's instability.

Standards

At the time of *Sol e Mar*'s sinking, the Coast Guard had "voluntary" standards for uninspected commercial fishing vessels like the *Sol e Mar*. According to longtime commercial fishing vessel safety advocate Richard Hiscock, "At the time the *Sol e Mar* departed Fairhaven in March 1990, it would have been required to be equipped with the following emergency rescue equipment: Two lifejackets and a deployable ring buoy; either three type B size 1 or one type B size II and one size I fire extinguishers." According to Hiscock, "the exposure suits could have substituted for the requirement for lifejackets."

A deeper analysis of these standards gives insight into critical questions and theories about what might have happened on board the sinking vessel immediately after Billy Hokanson's distress call was issued.

Why did young Hokanson get only one short, four-second radio distress call out to the Coast Guard and other nearby would-be rescuers? Providence inspectors determined the *Sol e Mar* "did not have a reserve source of electrical power independent of the vessel's main electrical installation."

Could the *Sol e Mar* have hung up on a wreck and the water quickly shorted out the primary source of power? But *Sol e Mar* had other emergency communications equipment onboard for just such an emergency.

According to Hiscock, "The Coast Guard did not require uninspected commercial fishing vessels to carry Emergency Position Indicating Radio Beacons (EPIRBs) until May 17, 1990." EPIRBs, when properly deployed from a sinking vessel, transmit a signal from which orbiting satellites could optimally provide a rough position of the distressed vessel within about ninety minutes of the time of the sinking. Coast Guard helicopters and boats were equipped with direction-finding equipment tuned to the EPIRB frequency, enabling rescuers to fine tune the location of the device once they got in the general area of the signal.

Hokanson's friends, however, knew the vessel did have an operable, Coast Guard–approved Class A EPIRB designed to break free from a sinking vessel and alert rescuers on frequency 121.5 MHz via orbiting satellites. Why didn't the Coast Guard receive any satellite distress signals?

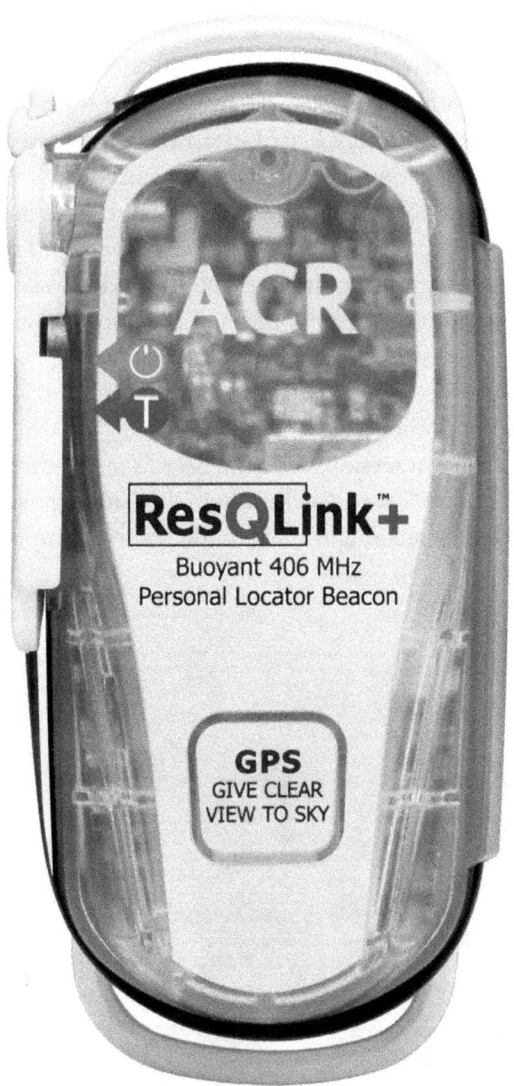

Modern satellite-capable personal locating beacons (PLBs) can be taken with crew members who abandon ships unlike 1990s-era EPIRBs, which sometimes became entangled with rigging and never deployed. *Image courtesy of ACR.*

The Sol e Mar Tragedy off Martha's Vineyard

Providence-based investigators determined Hokanson had a single EPIRB, or emergency beacon, mounting bracket inside the *Sol e Mar*'s wheelhouse. Inside bracket mountings were typical where boat captains were concerned about theft while the vessel was in port. After all, emergency beacons were expensive. Sometimes, marine investigators of the time found properly mounted EPIRBs with dead batteries—"too expensive to replace the batteries" was a frequent lament from fishermen.

At the time, Coast Guard personnel encouraged fishermen to have two sets of mounting brackets, one inside the wheelhouse for when the vessel was in port to prevent pilferage and a second bracket outside for when the vessel got underway. The Coast Guard did receive an EPIRB distress signal a week after the sinking, but the device was unregistered and did not remain operational long enough to be pinpointed and recovered.

But even with these challenges, investigators knew Hokanson had personal flotation devices (PFDs), life jackets and immersion suits onboard. Why weren't they used?

An immersion suit from *Sol e Mar* was discovered at sea south of Martha's Vineyard two weeks after the sinking, so investigators knew that the Hokansons might have made some attempt to don rescue gear. They knew

A Coast Guard crew in cold-weather gear boards a fishing vessel. *Image courtesy of U.S. Coast Guard.*

this to be a concerted effort, since Hokanson routinely and unfortunately had, according to Coast Guard reports, kept his PFDs and survival suits stored below decks in plastic bags. Family members and part-time crewman Randy Oliveira disputed this aspect of the report and indicated, "Hokey kept his PFDs up in the pilothouse. They would have been readily accessible."

Complicating matters more, 1990 Coast Guard Marine Safety investigators determined the *Sol e Mar* crew "did not conduct drills to ensure that the crew was adequately trained in their duties in the event of emergencies." But according to safety advocate Richard Hiscock, the requirements for instructions, drills and safety orientation briefings for vessels like *Sol e Mar* didn't take effect until 1991. "In 1991, the master of a vessel such as *Sol e Mar* would have been required to ensure that each individual on board was given instruction and that drills [were] conducted so that individuals [were] familiar with their duties and responses to the following contingencies: abandoning ship, fires, flooding, launch[ing] survival craft, don[ning] immersion suits and donning firefighting equipment." But none of these items were required until months after *Sol e Mar* sank.

RESCUE ANALYSIS

Nearly simultaneously to the Providence report, Rear Admiral Richard Rybacki, then commander of the First Coast Guard District (for the geographic area from Toms River, New Jersey, to Canada) issued his findings from an informal search and rescue case study that examined the broader issues in the *Sol e Mar* sinking. In a July 11, 1990 letter incident report, Rybacki tackled critical operational and legal issues in the *Sol e Mar* case, including his own Coast Guard personnel's actions and procedures at the time. Pointing the finger squarely at the hoax caller, Rybacki indicated, "This truly unfortunate incident reveals the necessity of ending the illegal use of the airwaves. It is readily apparent that the hoax call received, less than two minutes after the SOL E MAR distress call, resulted in misinterpretation of the facts by the SDO (Senior Duty Officer) at Group Woods Hole." The admiral's report promulgated "additional guidance regarding the prosecution of hoax cases, now necessitating a more senior level review for each call." The district commander's report suggested that "guidance in effect at the time of this incident was sufficient to assist watch standers in taking the appropriate action. The guidance clearly indicates that all distress or potential distress calls should be reported to the First District Operations Center (in Boston)."

In essence, Admiral Rybacki was suggesting the watch standers at Group Woods Hole had acted contrary to existing policy on the night of March 25, 1990. They should have consulted with more senior officials at the admiral's own Boston command center. But would the Boston controllers have acted any differently than the Woods Hole watch standers if the group watch stander reported what he believed to be true at the time? In a June 1990 interview with *Commercial Fisheries News*, Rybacki "stressed that the study revealed no negligence on the part of the Coast Guardsmen involved and that no disciplinary action was anticipated."

Admiral Rybacki worried that these "irresponsible calls endanger Coast Guard men and women who often risk their lives for what they think is a rescue mission." But there was also a more insidious aspect to hoax calls that worried the Coast Guard's leadership.

Coast Guard officials were worried that a "boy who cried wolf" atmosphere was developing among response teams. Rybacki intoned that "because of the frequency of hoaxes recently, I'm worried that our people will begin doubting the legitimacy of real calls for assistance, which could inhibit the enthusiasm and dedication of our crews."

Changes in Protocol

So what was the Coast Guard's response to the *Sol e Mar* tragedy and the ever-increasing spate of hoax calls?

Within three days after the *Sol e Mar* search was suspended, new search and rescue procedures were adopted at the First Coast Guard District, which, according to Admiral Rybacki, "require a distress response be made in all cases while it is being evaluated, to eliminate confusion, to streamline our initial response to all distress calls, and to elevate the authority to suspend such hoaxes to the search and rescue coordinator at the District."

So what difference would these changes have made in the context of the *Sol e Mar* case? The change of policy would have had a twofold effect. First, it would have required Group Woods Hole to have proceeded with regard to what they believed to be the hoax case as if it were a legitimate call for help. What might this have meant in terms of Hokey and Billy Hokanson?

Second, in the most optimistic of circumstances, the new procedure might have caused the group watch standers, the only location to have recordings at the time, to review their recording tapes of the two calls and confer with the two other rescue stations that had received the original call from *Sol e Mar*. But they could only have done this if they somehow could have discerned the name *Sol e Mar* from Billy Hokanson's original badly garbled cry for help on the tape.

If rescuers had the context of the name *Sol e Mar*, they still wouldn't know exactly where to search because Billy Hokanson was unable to give the vessel's position. However, the Coast Guard did have a crude 240-degree line of bearing from Nantucket's Brant Point station. The bearing, according to Coast Guard documents at the time, was only good to plus or minus five degrees of accuracy.

The name of the vessel in distress would have allowed Coast Guard personnel to tailor their Urgent Marine Information Broadcast (UMIB) to include the name *Sol e Mar* in the alerting broadcast that solicited other mariners' assistance. This might have caused the nearby fishing vessel *Resolute*, which had rendezvoused with the *Sol e Mar* forty-five minutes prior to the hoax call, to give the Coast Guard some idea of where to send help. Or even for the *Resolute* or the fishing vessel *Minflicka*, which newspaper reports indicated was within two miles of the *Sol e Mar*, to render aid and begin to search in the area.

But the *Resolute* and *Minflicka* were not apparently monitoring distress channel 16 at the time anyway. During an April 2, 1990 meeting at the Skipper Motor Inn, fishermen who were close to the *Sol e Mar* the night of the sinking asked Captain Anthony Pettit, the Group Woods Hole commander, "Why didn't the Coast Guard come on the mariners channel with the vessel in distress?" According to Ellen Ouellette's personal journal, Pettit told the audience that "that was not the Coast Guard's job; it was the fishermen's job to stay tuned to their [distress] channel."

In Rybacki's June 1990 interview, he "acknowledged that in hindsight different decisions could have been made and pointed out the district's change in how it will respond to suspected hoax calls." He also questioned "why there had been no fishing vessel response to radio attempts by two Coast Guard stations to reach a vessel in distress. We needed each other's help in this situation."

In a September 1990 *Commercial Fisheries News* article, Scituate draggerman Frank Mirachi intoned, "What happened in the case of the *Sol e Mar* was an outrage. Fishermen are not exempt from criticism and have had their consciousness raised by the incident. We're keeping better track of each other and monitoring channel 16."

Mirachi went on to explain how difficult it is for fishermen to monitor channel 16 and be "constantly subjected to the incessant chatter coming over the hailing/distress frequency." Federal officials knew of the frequency congestion and subsequently scheduled tests on channel 9 that would be designated a hailing frequency, freeing up channel 16 for exclusive emergency.

IDEAL CIRCUMSTANCES

Under ideal circumstances, if the Coast Guard had been able to quickly clean up Billy's original tape of the call for help, discern *Sol e Mar*'s name and quickly issue a specific UMIB, and if *Resolute* had communicated the position where the two boats had rendezvoused, then a Coast Guard helicopter could have been dispatched from nearby Otis Air Base on Cape Cod or a motor lifeboat sent from Menemsha, Martha's Vineyard.

The helicopter, on fifteen-minute standby launch status, could have then flown to Nantucket and proceeded down the rough 240-degree line of bearing from there, or it could have flown to the last known position of the *Resolute*–*Sol e Mar* rendezvous and begun a search. Discounting any search time, an optimum solution for both the Coast Guard helicopter, the Menemsha motor lifeboat and nearby fishing vessels was approximately thirty to forty-five minutes.

If, if, if, if—all of this is unlikely, however, because the state of Coast Guard technology at the time (discussed in Chapter 7) was such that it took three hours to clean up the tape of Billy Hokanson's cry for help and determine the contents. The nearby fishing vessels were also not monitoring channel 16, as required by FCC regulations. Since the fishermen weren't listening to channel 16—where the Coast Guard was hailing, "Vessel calling the Coast Guard, come in, over" in response to Billy's garbled distress call—the fishermen couldn't connect the Coast Guard's calls to the distress call that three rescue stations and a marine surveyor on Cuttyhunk did hear.

TICKTOCK, THE HYPOTHERMIA CLOCK

Most importantly and unfortunately, hypothermia concerns for Hokey and Billy Hokanson—both reasonably good swimmers and certified divers, according to Ellen Ouellette—began the moment they were immersed in the forty-three-degree Atlantic Ocean. Rescuers know that neither Hokey nor Billy was able to don his immersion suit, which is designed to protect the skin from cold water, since two suits were eventually recovered weeks after the vessel sank.

So how long might Hokey and Billy have survived while their would-be rescuers were trying to figure out whether or not they had a real case?

Before that question can be answered, evaluators of this grisly process have to make some assumptions. The first relates to whether the Hokansons were immersed or submerged in the water. Presuming both father and son had jumped free of any entangling hazards as the vessel sank and kept their heads out of the water, then they were "immersed" instead of being submerged.

Second, physicians familiar with cold water have to discuss the body's physiological reactions to being immersed. The first phenomenon Hokey and Billy Hokanson would have faced was "cold-shock," or the body's reaction to being suddenly dunked in cold water. Occurring immediately on entry to water colder than sixty-eight degrees, cold-shock can last up to two minutes. This phenomenon, caused by the "stimulation of nerve endings on the back and chest, can cause a sudden gasp reflex, hyperventilation, difficulty holding your breath, tachycardia (rapid heart rate) and hypertension (elevated blood pressure)," according to Al Steinman, former U.S. Coast Guard director of Health and Safety. The "colder the water, the stronger the reaction," Steinman noted.

The immediate threat here is if either of the Hokinsons' heads were under water during this initial gasp reflex, it could have led to immediate death by drowning. Secondarily, according to Steinman, cold water immersion leads to an "extreme decrease in breath-holding time that accompanies the hyperventilation—which can also lead to drowning if the victims need to escape from an enclosed space (e.g. capsized vessel). Finally, some victims suffer cardiac arrest or abnormal heart rhythms (which can lead to unconsciousness and drowning) because of a sudden increase in heart rate and blood pressure," Steinman asserts.

Presuming both the Hokansons were able to calm themselves sufficiently during this two-minute critical period of cold shock, evaluators have to discuss the gradual deleterious effects of cold water on the body. As blood leaves the body's extremities and seeks to warm the internal organs, manual dexterity of the arms, legs and hands begins to deteriorate in the period two to fifteen minutes after immersion. According to Steinman, "swim failure, the loss of manual dexterity, loss of functionality, and muscle cramping" are all typical as time progresses.

Steinman notes, "Swimming in cold water is difficult, even for good swimmers, and some people actually drown during this period because they are unable to maintain airway freeboard with effective use of their arms and legs, which is critical throughout all phases of the cold-water immersion period." Any type of physical activity, especially swimming while immersed, speeds the onset of these symptoms and hypothermia, as the activity drives blood back to the extremities, rapidly cooling the body and causing exhaustion.

According to Steinman, "Victims immersed in cold water who survive the initial cold water shock can extend their chances of survival by limiting their activity." Presuming the Hokansons survived this pivotal first fifteen-minute period that leaves many others in similar circumstances functionally disabled, what would they do next?

After about thirty minutes from the time of immersion, the body's temperature begins to significantly decline. Hypothermia begins once the body's core temperature reaches ninety-five degrees Fahrenheit. Death by hypothermia is not an exact science.

The lowest core temperature from which a victim of hypothermia has recovered is 55.4 degrees Fahrenheit in 2010, when a Swedish seven-year-old girl was resuscitated. On Christmas Day 2010, the seven-year-old girl was found in the ocean on Sweden's western coast. She showed no signs of life when recovered. According to Dr. Otterlind, a local physician, "A few circumstances, including the fact that she was already cold when she landed in the water, helped make her recovery possible. The brain can survive longer without oxygen if the body temperature is lower. Her age also helped. "Children usually have better chances of surviving a situation like this compared to adults. The young, developing brain is a lot better at compensating for possible damage."

Survival time predictive models exist for hypothermia but depend on myriad variables, including the victim's size; age; what they were wearing, including PFDs; previous medical history; the sea state; water temperature; whether a life raft was available; and the level of activity for the immersed person. PFDs might keep some portion of the body out of the water and limit the need for physical activity, prolonging life. High sea states might continually cause water to lap over the top of individuals treading water, accelerating cooling and reducing longevity. "Large, fat people cool much more slowly than tall, lanky people," according to Dr. Steinman.

So we may never know when the Hokansons died or even if they escaped from the *Sol e Mar*, but hypothermia probably wasn't a problem until after about thirty minutes of immersion. At this point, according to Steinman, "The body would maintain blood flow to vital organs (heart, lungs, brain, liver and kidneys). Despite the body's defensive mechanisms, heat continues to flow from the body to the surrounding water." The body attempts to counteract the loss of heat by increasing metabolic rate. The body begins to shiver in order to produce more heat. And the body's shivering response, according to Steinman, "becomes maximal around a core temperature of 95 degrees Fahrenheit." As the core temperature continues to decrease, shivering and muscle coordination all eventually decline. In some cases, the loss of muscle coordination can lead to death from drowning long before significant hypothermia sets in.

For most individuals, continued loss of core temperature due to immersion further impairs judgment and speech, fosters irrational thought processes and promotes eventual loss of consciousness near eighty-six degrees Fahrenheit. Had the Hokansons survived the initial sinking, death would have been slow and difficult.

Most people don't understand that a person exposed to cold-water immersion can still die, even after being rescued. The phenomenon, called "peri-rescue," can be observed in the 2013 blockbuster hit *Captain Phillips*, in which Captain Rich Phillips from the merchant vessel *Maersk Alabama* is held captive by Somali pirates for an extended period under the imminent threat of death. After being dramatically rescued by SEAL Team 6 members and crew of the USS *Bainbridge*, Phillips is rushed to the navy ship's sick bay, where he is clearly in shock, blubbering, hardly able to speak or respond to his rescuers.

Peri-rescue or circum-rescue shock is a very dangerous period for survivors, and unless treated appropriately, they can perish as a result of sudden loss of blood pressure due to shock.

Admiral's Analysis

In an interview almost a year after the tragedy, Rybacki clarified his earlier declaration about the sufficiency of the preexisting Coast Guard procedures by saying, "We made it very clear that any case involving a hoax or one that was suspected as a hoax would be responded to as in any case." The new clarifications were important enough or unclear enough to have precipitated a district-wide rollout where "several district wide meetings with group commanders" were held after the tragedy. The admiral's report went on

The Sol e Mar Tragedy off Martha's Vineyard

to acknowledge that the "District SAR [search and rescue] plan indicates that a hoax is a type of case where all factors must be evaluated prior to categorizing the case as such. Up until that final evaluation is made, it is evident that the call is clearly either a distress or a potential distress and should be reported to the Operations Center." So if the district's SAR plan provided adequate guidance and direction about potential hoax calls, what caused the Group Woods Hole watch standers to become confused?

Other Factors

Despite the March time frame, one of the slowest times of the year for rescue cases in the area, and the 9:18 p.m. hour of Hokanson's call, the admiral asked his audience to believe that "group communications watch standers have far too many duties. The watch standers can no longer perform their primary duty, which is to guard communications distress channels."

Commander Mike DaPonte, a former Group Portland (Maine) duty officer, supported the admiral's supposition and clarified that the time of year or the time of day made little difference with regard to how slow or busy the radios were in the communications center. "You could walk in to the communications center at the height of the summer SAR season and hear a pin drop. Or, you could walk in there after midnight in the dead of winter and not hear yourself think."

The admiral's report went on: "One person [of the] Group Woods Hole communications watch is responsible for maintaining a listening watch on 12 different speakers. It is nearly impossible to determine from which speaker a signal has originated, unless the watch standers are directly in front of that particular console." Watch standers had additional duties, including operating radio teletypes, routing and filing formal messages and answering telephones, as well as managing an entirely separate set of classified communications equipment.

Admiral Rybacki's report continued: "Listening to distress frequencies is the foundation of the Coast Guard's SAR mission." In its final sections, the admiral called for a comprehensive review of the communications watch to "determine if Coast Guard units are adequately staffed with radiomen to ensure completion of all necessary missions and whether or not the equipment is properly situated so as to maximize their ability to listen to the various distress frequencies. 'This case is closed.'"

THE SOL E MAR TRAGEDY OFF MARTHA'S VINEYARD

A Congressman's Ire

But the case of *Sol e Mar* was far from closed for Congressman Gerry Studds, who was angry and called for hearings at Woods Hole shortly after Rybacki's report was promulgated. The Subcommittee on Coast Guard and Navigation, Committee on Merchant Marine and Fisheries, headed by Congressmen Billy Tausin and Gerry Studds, scheduled an oversight hearing at Woods Hole for July 23, 1990. Tausin and Studds were coming to Woods Hole to receive testimonials from the Coast Guard, local fishermen and others concerning HR 4632, a bill that would "increase the penalties against those who make false distress calls to the Coast Guard."

This was powerful legislation, but Congressman Studds's greatest insight to the *Sol e Mar* tragedy came before the official hearings at the Woods Hole Oceanographic Institute during a brief tour of the Coast Guard's Woods Hole Communications Center—the same communications center that had mishandled Billy Hokanson's distress call months earlier.

After witnessing a single radio operator, clearly overwhelmed, attempting to monitor twelve separate radio frequencies simultaneously, Studds commented, "It was a room full of noise. There's no way on earth a brief and garbled radio distress message as came from the *Sol e Mar* could have been understood in that room.

"The scene we saw in the watch room at Woods Hole really was a shocker. It was amazing that any calls are accurately heard and understood given that poor watch officer is affected by up to a dozen radios blaring at him and without the most sophisticated pieces of equipment."

Studds also stated that the rescue stations involved in the *Sol e Mar* case did not have state-of-the-art direction-finding equipment and actually "were using World War II equipment. And the direction-finding equipment, which with the ability to record, replay and clean up and understand messages, were [*sic*] not what it ought to have been." Studds proposed legislation that authorized the Coast Guard up to $2 million to acquire radio direction-finding equipment to enhance its ability to locate and identify mariner distress calls.

After the *Sol e Mar* hearing, the FCC also began a series of tests "to clear channel 16 of leisure calls" and began experimenting with the use of channel 9 VHF-FM as an alternative frequency for less important conversations.

Almost a year after the *Sol e Mar* sinking, Congressman Studds gave a March 21, 1991 interview for the *Barnacle*, a Fairhaven, Massachusetts newspaper. "Sometimes when you have a human tragedy the least you can do to honor the memory of those who were lost is to learn from that experience and see to it to minimize the chances of it ever being repeated."

Sol e Mar Timeline for Tragedy

March 22, 1990

Billy and Hokey Hokanson depart Boston in the fishing vessel *Sol e Mar* for a five-day fishing trip off Martha's Vineyard.

March 25, 1990

8:30 p.m.: Dave Butcher from the fishing vessel *Resolute* rendezvous with *Sol e Mar* and passes Billy Hokanson a piece of equipment.

9:18 p.m.: Billy sends a four-second, heavily garbled Mayday heard by three Coast Guard stations and a Sea Tow operator on Cuttyhunk. Nobody who hears the call initially recognizes Billy's voice or hears the name *Sol e Mar*. Coast Guard Station Brant Point Nantucket obtains a 240-degree line of bearing on the call. Coast Guard stations attempt to make contact with the caller without success.

9:20 p.m.: A hoax caller then says, "SOS, I'm sinking" followed by laughter. This misleads Coast Guard rescuers into believing the hoax caller was Billy Hokanson, despite clues to indicate that there were two calls. Later analysis would show the hoax caller was transmitting his prank call on low power from the Woods Hole area.

March 27, 1990

The date Billy and Hokey originally planned to return to Fairhaven, Massachusetts.

March 29, 1990

9:30 p.m.: The *Sol e Mar* is reported overdue by a family member. A massive search ensues covering a wide area because Billy Hokanson's distress call and Brant Point's direction-finding bearing have not yet been linked to the case.

April 1, 1990

1:40 p.m.: A Cuttyhunk Sea Tow operator calls the Coast Guard and reports hearing a March 25 distress call. Coast Guard tapes are cleaned up, and Billy Hokanson's distress call now clearly indicates, "This is the fishing vessel Sol e Mar. This is a Mayday. This is the fishing vessel Sol e Mar; we're sinking. We need help now!"
10:00 p.m.: The Coast Guard suspends the active search for Sol e Mar.

April 24, 1990

1:00 p.m.: Twelve volunteers in the borrowed research vessel Marlin find the Sol e Mar in 138 feet of water seven miles southwest of Martha's Vineyard, very close to the position where Billy Hokanson had received a piece of equipment from the fishing vessel Resolute the night of the sinking.

May 6, 1990

Hokey and Billy are eulogized by more than five hundred family members and friends at the Seamen's Bethel in New Bedford, Massachusetts.

July 23, 1990

A congressional hearing is held at Group Woods Hole and the Woods Hole Oceanographic Institute in Woods Hole, Massachusetts. Congressmen Studds and Tausin observe a Coast Guard radio watch stander overwhelmed by his multiple duties and using inadequate World War II-era equipment.

November 1990

The Studds Act is passed. The act creates a tough new anti-hoax law, making it a federal crime punishable by up to six years in prison to prank the Coast Guard.

5
NEXT OF KIN (NOK) PROCEDURES

Today's Coast Guard next of kin (NOK) procedures in the National Search and Rescue Addendum clearly define responsibility and sensitivity requirements when guard members interact with family members who have lost or are thought to have lost loved ones in maritime accidents:

> *The District Commander shall ensure the greatest possible sensitivity in interacting with family and friends of victims during the conduct of SAR cases where the Coast Guard is the lead agency. Sector Commanders shall personally ensure that notifications are made and interaction established with the NOK at the earliest possible time.*

Rear Admiral Rich Rybacki, the 1990 Coast Guard District One commander, played an active role in interacting with some Hokanson family members. After the Coast Guard figured out what had happened with the hoax call, Rybacki invited family members to the Skipper Bar and Grille in Fairhaven, Massachusetts, a small community not far from New Bedford along I-195, for a briefing and to try to answer questions. He was prepared to take the heat. And there was plenty of it.

Unfortunately, as Hokanson family members were waiting for the start of the meeting, Mrs. Francis Bagge, cousin of William Sr., overheard two senior Coast Guard officials talking to each other, allegedly saying, "I hope they have a good lawyer because we've been through this before." One official also remarked to Ellen Ouellette's brother-in-law, Raymond Oliveira, "Man to man, we screwed-up." What the Coast Guardsmen were implying was that the Coast Guard had liability in the *Sol e Mar* case.

This set the tone for the meeting and discussions about why the Coast Guard had not searched when Billy Hokanson had issued a Mayday. Ellen Ouellette thought that if "she were in a similar circumstance where she had worked at her hospital and a patient or other person were to cry for help, she would be duty-bound to try to find that person," meaning the Coast Guard had not done everything it could do for her former husband and only son.

Ouellette pointedly asked Rear Admiral Rybacki if the Coast Guard had gone out, what would have happened. "The Coast Guard had a direction-finding line of bearing from Nantucket," she said. The admiral, according to Ouellette, hung his head and could not respond. "He didn't know how to answer me."

Ouellette pressed the admiral for answers, further inquiring, "How long would it have taken the Coast Guard to get on scene?" The admiral, according to Ouellette, responded, "About thirty minutes, maybe."

In a later conversation with the Coast Guard, when the family knew they weren't going to recover their loved ones' bodies, they received information that the fishing vessel *Dianna* from Westport, Massachusetts, had spotted a large black dog floating near Nomans Island. According to Ellen Ouellette, "My husband Eddie called the Coast Guard Station, and they said that they wouldn't go out there and pick it up because they don't retrieve dead bodies."

The modern-day NOK policy also goes on to suggest that a single family point of contact should be designated to focus communications and ensure all family members know how to direct their inquiries and limit the number of calls received by operational Coast Guard units. But these procedures were not yet fully developed in 1990 when the *Sol e Mar* case was ongoing. Exacerbating the situation was a complicated web of Hokanson family members, including a mother/grandmother, four brothers/uncles, a daughter/sister, an ex-wife/mother and two girlfriends. The strongest voice—the reporting source for the overdue vessel and ex-wife and mother to the lost fishermen, Ellen Ouellette—was unofficially designated by some family members and the Coast Guard as the family spokesperson.

But without the service's protocols that would follow years later to accommodate all family members, even those not nearby, some family members were left with a void of information. Cheryl Best, Hokey's daughter and Billy's sister, would be troubled for years to come based on a lack of information at a critical time of her grieving. Even though she was somewhat comforted in knowing her dad "loved the ocean and its beauty and he died doing what he loved," she needed answers to some nagging questions.

In a letter to the Coast Guard on August 17, 1992, almost two and a half years after the *Sol e Mar* sank, Best wrote, "It's been a long and rocky road getting my life in order since my dad's death. I would just like to know what happened. It's hard when you don't have any answers and don't know what happened"

Cheryl went on to ask the Coast Guard several questions owing to the fact that "all information went to my father's ex-wife, Ellen Ouellette. I never received any information." She wondered "if any of the dogs' bodies were recovered? Was a survival suit found my father's? Did you ever find out who made the hoax call? Did the person making the hoax call hear my brother making the SOS call?"

Adding frustration to her angst was the Coast Guard's previous lack of response: "Twice I wrote letters to the Coast Guard. One time, someone called and asked for my address, he said he had a response to my letters. I never received any response. What happened?"

In an August 28, 1992 response, Group Woods Hole deputy commander Tom Landvogt told Ms. Best: "We never did find out who made the 'hoax' call, so we do not know if that person heard the SOLEMAR's [*sic*] call for help." Commander Landvogt referred Best to his senior command, the First Coast Guard District legal office and the Freedom of Information Act (FOIA) process.

The Coast Guard was essentially telling Best that she could go help herself by contacting the Coast Guard's lawyers and pursuing a set of fairly impersonal processes designed for the masses. According to the Department of Justice website:

> *Enacted on July 4, 1966, and taking effect one year later, the Freedom of Information Act (FOIA) provides that any person has a right, enforceable in court, to obtain access to federal agency records, except to the extent that such records (or portions of them) are protected from public disclosure by one of nine exemptions or by one of three special law enforcement record exclusions. A FOIA request can be made for any agency record.*

Cheryl Best never applied for information through the FOIA process and would not get her questions answered for decades. And it would be six and a half more years before the Coast Guard would develop enhanced next of kin procedures to improve the flow of information to family members whose loved ones were missing at sea. New NOK procedures would follow after the 1997 sailing vessel *Morning Dew* tragedy off Charleston, South Carolina.

THE 1997 MORNING DEW TRAGEDY

The *Morning Dew* case shared many of the same unfortunate details as the *Sol e Mar* case. It began on December 29, 1997. At 2:17 a.m. the U.S. Coast Guard Group Charleston, South Carolina, received the following emergency call: "May...MAYDAY, U.S. Coast Guard come in." The call came from the young, frightened voice of thirteen-year-old Daniel Cornett on VHF-FM radio distress channel 16. At U.S. Coast Guard Group Charleston, this particular three-second-long radio call was received and automatically recorded by the Stancil recorder, a device designed to preserve critical radio messages.

Unfortunately, the Coast Guard's sole radio watch stander was seventeen feet away, just inside the communications center, refilling his coffee mug. Following standard radio telephone protocol, the radio watch stander responded just fourteen seconds later: "Vessel calling Coast Guard, this is Coast Guard Group Charleston, over." But there would be no more radio calls from the thirty-four-foot sailboat *Morning Dew* on this fateful night.

The watch stander quickly returned to the normal humdrum of off-season and late-night quietude and routine. Investigators believe that the boat's crew—Michael Cornett, forty-nine, skipper of the *Morning Dew* and father of crewmates young Daniel and his sixteen-year-old brother, Paul, and their cousin fourteen-year-old Bobby Hurd Jr.—had just been thrown overboard by the force of the sailboat's crashing into the rock jetty leading into the port of Charleston, South Carolina.

Almost four hours after the initial call, the inbound Japanese car carrier *Pearl Ace* reported hearing cries from the water. The Coast Guard radio watch stander, not previously attaching value to the 2:17 a.m. distress call from Daniel Cornett, did not link the two situations. The senior watch standers, unfortunately, also muffed this last opportunity to render aid and did not launch any Coast Guard resources.

At 11:00 a.m., a couple walking on the beach on Sullivan's Island saw young Daniel Cornett's lifeless body adrift just offshore, clad only in his boxer shorts. A horseshoe-style life preserver with *Morning Dew* stenciled on its side also washed ashore. At approximately 1:15 p.m., Paul Cornett's lifeless body was recovered two miles from the jetty. Michael Cornett's body washed ashore on Sullivan's Island more than three weeks later, on January 23, 1998.

According to newspaper accounts, near midnight on the day following the *Morning Dew*'s sinking, Libby Cornett, Michael's wife and mother to Daniel and Paul Cornett, was roused from sleep at her mother's home in Canal Point, Florida. Libby Cornett listened to Bobby Hurd's family pastor in shock as he inquired, "Have you heard if any more bodies have washed up?" This was Libby Cornett's first notice of the *Morning Dew* disaster. Citing the need for an exhaustive ongoing investigation, it would be weeks before the Coast Guard would make family notifications about the true circumstances of the events of the night of December 29, 1997, including the existence of the 2:17 a.m. cry for help. Among the many changes that would be promulgated in the wake of the *Morning Dew* case were clear mandates for next of kin protocols that require immediate, face-to-face briefings and regular updates from senior officials during and at specified stages of the case.

The pain and anguish that some Hokanson family members experienced for years and that the Cornett and Hurd family members experienced for months after their tragedies as a result of incomplete and untimely communications from the Coast Guard could never be fixed. But among the many sweeping changes that evolved after the *Morning Dew* incident were enhanced operational and family support services, including comprehensive NOK procedures.

6

THE STUDDS ACT AND HOAX CALLS PAST AND PRESENT

The Coast Guard was two hundred years old in 1990, the year that Coast Guard Group Woods Hole watch standers were deceived by a cruel radio hoax caller and the *Sol e Mar* sank. The hoax caller caused the guard to incorrectly link his false transmission with young Billy Hokanson's earlier urgent cry for help. Hoax calls in 1990 were defined as "false incident reports which are made with the sole intent of deceiving the Coast Guard or any other agency." Shortly after the *Sol e Mar* tragedy, the Coast Guard began to collect hoax call information for the first time since the nearshore VHF-FM National Distress System (NDS) was introduced in 1970 to respond to mariners in distress. The NDS was a network of VHF-FM radio towers designed to monitor distress frequencies within twenty miles of U.S. shorelines. Approximately 90 percent of all distress calls received by the Coast Guard were transmitted in this area.

In a prepared statement to Congressman Gerry Studds, who represented the Tenth Congressional District that included the Cape and Islands and New Bedford, and others at the Woods Hole Oceanographic Institute on July 23, 1990, Rear Admiral Richard I. Rybacki spoke to the House Subcommittee on Coast Guard and Navigation about hoax cases. The admiral summarized the previous fiscal year's hoax cases and indicated there had been just eighteen false distress calls.

The admiral commented: "This is an estimate because the computerized case accounting system we have does not have a category for such incidents. However, in this fiscal year, beginning October 1, 1990, we have had 97 false distress or hoax cases, through July 12, and we have just begun the heavy boating season." Sadly, Rybacki also mentioned that the Coast Guard "had so many that we have had to manually augment the case accounting system to document such incidents."

Hokey and Billy Hokanson weren't the only people to have died as a result of cruel hoaxes perpetrated against the Coast Guard in 1990. According to the *Ludington, Ohio News*, "a fourteen-year-old Lorain boy died in Lorath Harbor, near the Coast Guard station while rescuers were eighteen miles away responding to a hoax." Fourteen-year-old Daniel Cortez died within sight of the local Coast Guard Station, according to Coast Guard chief petty officer Robert Bradford: "While we were searching, the drowning happened. We could've been there in three minutes if we were in station."

The distant caller had a child's voice but said, "Mayday...our boat is sinking," Bradford said. "We sent a 41-foot patrol boat out to investigate as soon as possible," Chief Warrant Officer Dan Waldschmidt said. "When you get a call like that you can't just say it's a hoax and not go." It took the Coast Guard forty-five minutes to ultimately determine the call was a prank, and Cortez drowned in the meantime.

In 1990, the Coast Guard received one thousand calls per week asking for assistance. Ten of those one thousand calls, or 1 percent, were false distress calls. But why was there such an increase in the number of hoax cases? In short, the notoriety of the *Sol e Mar* case had brought out a special breed of miscreant—copy cats eager to claim some portion of the limelight in the shadow of the recent tragedy. On April 11, 1990, just sixteen days after the *Sol e Mar* case, the Coast Guard responded to a report of distress from a vessel calling itself the *Sun and Sea*. The Coast Guard determined the case was another false distress call, and later, someone pointed out "Sun and Sea" translates in Portuguese to *Sol e Mar*. Each of the false distress cases came with a price. The *Sun and Sea* hoax case cost the government almost $10,000.

Again on April 20, 1990, a hoax caller declared distress using the vessel name *Margaret Marie*. This search case cost taxpayers almost $18,000. False distress or hoax calls waste taxpayers' dollars at an extraordinary rate.

According to Mark Forest, Congressman Studds's 1990 representative on the Cape and liaison to the region's fishing community: "Any time there is a loss of life in the fishing community, it will always have a very powerful impact to the people of the Cape and Islands. Fishermen are a very special breed around here. They and their families command a great deal of respect. But this specific case, *Sol e Mar*, was due to a hoax call, a prank, which made it very disturbing."

The Sol e Mar Tragedy off Martha's Vineyard

2014 Hourly Rates for Coast Guard Cutters, Boats and Aircrafts

Boats	Rate
Motor lifeboats	$4,189
Rubber boats	$1,617
Utility boat	$2,739
Small utility boat	$3,275
Aircraft	**Rate**
Helicopter HH60J	$13,880
Helicopter HH65	$9,855
Jet	$11,299
Cutters	**Rate**
Patrol boat 110 WPB	$3,452
Patrol boat	$2,577

Courtesy U.S. Coast Guard

Studds, according to Forest, "was the co-author of the 200 Mile Magnuson Fisheries Conservation Law and he had a strong connection to the fishing community. To Gerry, something needed to be done about this. Action was needed. He wanted a lot of attention on the case."

Alongside Studds's effort, Fairhaven advocates and friends collected 1,657 signatures from local fishermen, businessmen and their families to ensure Hokey and Billy's case got the attention it deserved. The petitioners "demand[ed] a Congressional hearing be initiated forthwith, in order to investigate the circumstances and to evaluate the facts surrounding the untimely sinking of the fishing vessel SOL E MAR in the waters south of Massachusetts and the subsequent loss of its Captain William Hokanson and his son William Hokanson, Jr. of Fairhaven, Massachusetts."

Studds held a Coast Guard and Navigation Subcommittee field hearing and brought members of Congress to Cape Cod on July 23, 1990. According to Forest, "The hearings and the press brought a lot of attention to the case, the dangers that fishermen face out at sea every day, and the challenges of the Coast Guard."

A few months later, Congressmen Studds and William "Billy" Tausin, representing the Third District in Louisiana, sponsored a new bill specifically addressing hoax calls perpetrated against Coast Guard rescuers. The bill, proposed to amend Section 88 of Title 14 United States Code, added paragraph (c) to Section 88, which would make willful hoax calls a federal crime punishable by imprisonment of up to six years with stiff civil penalties up to $250,000 and made it possible for the Coast Guard to recoup its costs for searches resulting from bogus calls.

Congressman Studds's anti-hoax bill, HR 4009/P.L 101-595 was formally passed in November 1990. The section (c) addition reads as follows:

(c) An individual who knowingly and willfully communicates a false distress message to the Coast Guard or causes the Coast Guard to attempt to save lives and property when no help is needed is—
(1) guilty of a class D felony;
(2) subject to a civil penalty of not more than $5,000; and
(3) liable for all costs the Coast Guard incurs as a result of the individual's action.

According to a November 21, 1990 *Boston Globe* article, the first individuals arrested after the Studds Act was enacted were two Stamford, Connecticut men, Michael Bova and Michael Messecar, both twenty-four, who were "apprehended by Stamford police, whose patrol car was guided to the suspects' car by a Coast Guard utility boat offshore about 3:00 a.m."

Coast Guard officials were led to suspect a hoax on November 20, 1990, by several clues. First, the position for the reported distress call was located on land not water. And according to guard officials, "The voice of the individual making the call was similar to 10 other hoax calls we have received in the past three months."

A darkened Coast Guard utility boat maneuvered in the area, watching the bearing of the hoax radio signal move around. According to Coast Guard officials, their boat saw a vehicle that looked like it was the one the signal was coming from, and the Stamford police sent a cruiser and arrested the individuals in the act.

The first individual prosecuted under what has become known as the Studds Act was Jorge Mestre, a Fairfax, Virginia amateur radio operator. Mestre pleaded guilty on February 12, 1993, to attempting to mislead rescuers on August 7, 1992. A *Washington Post* article reported that Mestre admitted to sending an "SOS signal saying that a boat with six people aboard was sinking off the Turks and Caicos Islands, according to court documents. The Coast Guard launched a full-scale rescue operation with ships and aircraft but found nothing." Mestre was convicted of communicating a false distress signal and agreed to surrender his radio license, sell his equipment and repay $50,000 to the Coast Guard.

According to current Coast Guard hoax-related websites, "In 1990, the first year we began keeping statistics on rescue hoaxes, U.S. Coast Guard units responded to 205 hoaxes. This number has increased steadily every year. The U.S. Coast Guard, along with the Federal Communications Commission and other agencies, is very concerned about the increasing number of search and rescue hoaxes."

In regard to a June 2012 case off Sandy Hook, New Jersey, that cost taxpayers more than $300,000, deputy commander Captain Greg Hitchen noted, "Hoax emergency calls like the one about a yacht explosion off New Jersey cost U.S. taxpayers millions of dollars a year, yet authorities who police the nation's coastlines acknowledge there's little they can do to prevent them."

The caller said in a calm, clear voice that "we have three deceased, nine injured aboard a sinking yacht called the *Blind Date* after an explosion on board. We have twenty-one souls on board, twenty in the water right now." The caller may or may not have known he had created a circumstance called a mass-casualty incident, which sends chills up responders' spines. Coast Guard cutters and aircraft and New York City police helicopters made a mad dash for the location, only to find nothing.

The article went on to indicate, "From the Canadian border down to Sandy Hook alone, the Coast Guard received 300 suspected hoax reports last year. Officials have to take such calls seriously, especially those like Monday's, which contained minute details, authorities said."

But why, despite the new technologies of the Rescue 21 near-shore VHF-FM rescue system, improvements in the Federal Communications Commission's (FCC) ability to track and fingerprint signals and a general reduction of the total number of calls to the Coast Guard for help, has the number of hoax calls continued to rise? In his July 23, 1990 testimony to Congress, Mr. Richard Smith from the Chief Field Operations Bureau of the FCC gave early and enduring insights: "Hoax calls, by their nature are very difficult to investigate. In the great majority of cases no one is caught due primarily to the short duration of the radio transmissions and the fact that they usually are non-repetitive. In those few instances where we have identified the person making the calls, they have generally turned out to be minors, often 12- or 13-year-olds."

Smith went on to point out that "a violation of the Communications Act was punishable criminally as a misdemeanor for a first offense with a fine up to $100,000 and/or up to one year in prison." He went on to indicate that "where the Justice department has been reluctant to press for criminal prosecution of minors, we have used FCC administrative sanctions and assessed their parent's [*sic*] fines." FCC administrative fines of up to $10,000 can be assessed for the transmission of false distress signals.

So what about the applicability of the Studds Act for juveniles, the main offenders of the distress frequencies? According to Captain John Astley, U.S. Coast Guard (Ret.), former chief of the Boston Coast Guard Legal office:

> *The Studds Act applies to juvenile offenders, but absent extraordinary circumstances, federal law defers to state prosecutions of youth offenders. That generally means that criminal offenses get handled under state processes, which allow for diversion programs for youths. When I was in District One* [Boston], *we pursued a federal hoax prosecution against two minors, but the U.S. Attorney's office wouldn't take the case and worked with state authorities to deal with the offenders.*

Astley went on to indicate:

> *We were so frustrated in our inability to deter hoax calls in New England that we researched whether we could hold the parents of a minor who made a hoax call liable for the Coast Guard's search costs, which as you know are quite extensive and allowed under the Studds Act. Unfortunately, our research indicated that, absent unique facts in which the parents had knowledge of the youth offender's actions, we would not likely prevail in such a civil lawsuit.*

In 1974, Congress adopted the Juvenile Justice and Delinquency Prevention Act, whose purpose was "to provide basic procedural rights for juveniles who came under federal jurisdiction and to bring federal procedures up to the standards set by various model acts, many state codes and court decisions. The purpose of the Act is to remove juveniles from the ordinary criminal process in order to avoid the stigma of a prior criminal conviction and to encourage treatment and rehabilitation."

But faced with the dilemma of the increasing number of hoax calls year after year and inconsistent and varied state laws for the main demographic juvenile hoax offenders, modern-day rescuers are also faced with different cultural and economic phenomena today than in 1990. A casual Google search of the web for the word "pranks" turned up over ten million hits. And many of those hits were linked to YouTube videos, pranking APPs, Prank Kits, television shows and commercial enterprises that have developed sophisticated mechanisms to take participants' money and glorify and normalize spoofing activities.

Is it any wonder today's Coast Guard is suffering from an onslaught to the rescue airwaves when America's youth can, for a small fee, amuse themselves with prankdial.com, enter a friend's phone number, choose from a selection of preformatted hoax calls, record the call for later amusement and listen in as their buddy is the recipient of verbal frustration?

7

THE COAST GUARD'S TECHNOLOGY IN 1990 AND NOW

On April 22, 1999, almost ten years after the *Sol e Mar* sinking, Admiral James Loy, then commandant of the Coast Guard, delivered remarks at the U.S. Naval Institute's 125th Annual Meeting at the U.S. Naval Academy in Annapolis, Maryland. The admiral, in an unprecedented move, deferred his annual State of the Coast Guard address in which he would normally have outlined his strategic direction for the entire service in all mission areas. Loy focused partially on the sad state of near-shore marine radio technologies.

Loy compared the public's ability to yell, "Fire!" into their telephones, leave their burning homes and have the fire departments respond a few minutes later with the Coast Guard's inadequate radio system. Analogizing the Coast Guard's 1950s vintage rescue radio system, he commented that if "you pick up the handset on your VHF-FM handset today, shout 'Fire!' and jump overboard, you could very likely drown or die of hypothermia."

The admiral went on to further indicate how the Coast Guard's operations centers "cannot enhance and replay audio signals, and they lack useful direction-finding equipment." Further, the commandant pointed out that "our search and rescue communications depend on the ability of people whose lives are in immediate peril to explain calmly their identity, their location, and the nature of their distress."

The commandant went on to articulate the Coast Guard's need for a "communications system that gives our watchstanders the ability to translate desperate 'Mayday' calls into effective action; a system that allows watchstanders to replay calls, slowing them down and adjusting the quality until the message can be understood, a system that determines and preserves an electronic fix every time a signal is received."

Admiral Loy finally invited serious self-introspection by the public and focused on the individual boater's responsibility for his own safety at sea. "We face a moral imperative to learn from the mistakes we observe," said the Coast Guard's commandant. He further stated that "we show the greatest respect for those who have been lost—especially for those who die unnecessarily—when we use the occasion of their deaths to prevent others from sharing their fates." The Coast Guard had gotten the message. Planning and resourcing for a truly capable and comprehensive near-shore radio distress system would now be forthcoming.

In related 1999 service-wide correspondence, Rear Admiral R.J. Casto, assistant commandant for acquisitions, directed the cooperation of Coast Guard field units about a "long awaited and vitally important National Distress and System Modernization Program (NDSMP)." Casto's message went on to set a schedule of visits that included Coast Guard Group Woods Hole, the area where the *Sol e Mar* had sunk in 1990.

This national distress program was scheduled to replace an older system that was originally implemented in 1970 and designed to capture near-shore distress calls within twenty miles of the coastline. The previous system was, according to Coast Guard records, "the primary means for mariners to contact the Coast Guard in a distress—over 20,000 distress calls are received yearly over this system. Of the 25 largest U.S. cities ranked by population in the 1990 census, 19 cities, i.e. 76 percent, are close to navigable waters and are within at least partial coverage of the system."

The original 1970 VHF-FM system had a service life of fifteen years and was a tired and incomplete system by the time the *Sol e Mar* sank on March 25, 1990. The Coast Guard's mission responsibilities had doubled, and the number of recreational boaters had also increased since the inception of the old system. Worse, there were sixty-eight known "black holes," or gaps, in the radio coverage areas, including the location where young Billy Hokanson made his ill-fated distress call.

Casto's $300 million VHF-FM replacement project would finally begin to address some of the flaws that remained in the area where the *Sol e Mar* sank. The Rescue 21 system was finally and fully implemented in Sector Southeastern New England (formerly Group Woods Hole) in 2010, twenty years after the *Sol e Mar* incident. "Groups" and later their replacement "Sectors" are the Coast Guard's near-shore command and control hubs for all coastal mission areas. The Rescue 21 system would make a repeat of the *Sol e Mar* tragedy much less likely.

According to Coast Guard literature, "Rescue 21, the Coast Guard's advanced command, control and direction-finding communications system, was created to better locate mariners in distress and save lives and property at sea and on navigable rivers. By harnessing state-of-the-market technology, Rescue 21 enables the Coast Guard to execute its search and rescue missions with greater agility and efficiency."

Further, "Rescue 21 can more accurately identify the location of callers in distress via towers that generate lines of bearing to the source of VHF radio transmissions, thereby significantly reducing search time. Rescue 21 extends coverage out to a minimum of 20 nautical miles from the coastline. It improves information sharing and coordination with the Department of Homeland Security and other federal, state and local first responders, and can also identify suspected hoax calls, conserving valuable response resources." The Rescue 21 system's ability to "identify hoax calls" refers to the capability to find the direction of a signal and alert an operator that its origin is on land versus coming from a vessel at sea.

First, beginning with a new antenna established on Peaked Hill, Martha's Vineyard, in 2000, the black hole, or coverage gap, that had hampered Billy Hokanson's 1990 distress call was largely fixed. After 2000, distress calls made off Nomans Island were no longer blocked by hills on Martha's Vineyard. While the quality of Billy Hokanson's call may have been improved slightly by the better-quality antenna, the new antenna did nothing to improve the Coast Guard's recording and direction-finding capabilities until a progression of local improvements and the final Rescue 21 field upgrades were made in 2010.

Billy's original call was heard by operators at three Coast Guard stations: Station Woods Hole, Station Menemsha (on Martha's Vineyard) and Station Brant Point (on Nantucket). Station Woods Hole was located fifty feet from its parent group at Woods Hole but had separate communications equipment. While the Group Woods Hole operations center radio watch stander did not hear Billy's call for help, the group was the only location to have the capability to record radio transmissions and did record *Sol e Mar*'s distress call.

Brant Point rescue station was the only station to have obtained a direction-finding line of bearing on Billy's call for help. Coast Guard direction-finding equipment at small rescue stations like Brant Point in 1990 was unfortunately akin to old-fashioned magnetic compasses, in which a radio signal received would "deflect" a needle toward the direction of the caller. The problem was there was no recording capability, either for the audio signal or the direction-finding compass bearing at the small stations. As soon as another radio call came in to the station, the original direction bearing for the last call was lost forever.

The *Sol e Mar* distress call was a perfect confluence of technology and human failures. One of the Coast Guard station watch standers who heard Billy's call for help indicated that the caller was "panicky, the voice was garbled and was very difficult to understand." The group radio watch stander, unfortunately, either did not hear Billy Hokanson's cry for help or was distracted with many other duties at the time.

While the three stations that had heard the call were immediately responding and making attempts to generically hail a vessel in distress, according to Coast Guard records, the hoax caller used a low-power transmission from somewhere in the Woods Hole area to make his deadly prank call.

Unfortunately, the Group and Station Woods Hole radio watch standers were the only ones with the capability to hear the hoax call, so when the Brant Point station later queried the group about Billy's distress call, the response, according to Coast Guard records, was, "Yeah, I heard it, and it's BS." The phone recording at the time indicated that Brant Point and the group then continued to discuss other things. Since the group watch stander apparently didn't actually hear the *Sol e Mar* distress call, he thought the Brant Point watch stander was referring to the later hoax call.

The Coast Guard's direction-finding capabilities in 1990 were pitiful. One of the techniques practiced in the 1990s as a result of the *Sol e Mar* case was that, when land-based prank calls were suspected, the Coast Guard auxiliarists would act as a poor man's radio direction-finding capability.

The Coast Guard Reserve Act of 1939 founded the service's reserve component, including its civilian volunteer segment. On February 19, 1941, Congress restructured the Coast Guard Reserves for wartime purposes and calved off the volunteer Coast Guard Auxiliary. Today's Coast Guard Auxiliary performs many of the same functions as its active-duty counterpart, excepting law enforcement and military duties.

In a throwback to World War II techniques, auxiliary Coast Guard members would operate in hoax call direction-finding teams of two members working from automobiles. Given a suspicion of a land-originated hoax call, teams would be mobilized to help find the source of the phony calls. A general land search area would be assigned to the auxiliarists based

The Sol e Mar Tragedy Off Martha's Vineyard

on crude lines of bearing from the nearby Coast Guard group. Multiple auxiliary teams would operate in search grids within the search area.

Each car would have three VHF-FM handheld radios. The first radio would have a normal, government-issued antenna. The second radio would have the antenna removed and replaced by a Number 2 lead pencil. The pencil would act as a makeshift antenna. The third and final radio would have no antenna whatsoever.

The concept allowed an individual mobile search unit to close in on a transmitting prank call knowing that if they could hear a suspect using just the radio with the pencil, they were within a city block of the source. And if they could hear a suspect with no antenna at all, they were really close, perhaps within a few hundred feet.

The proverbial fly in the ointment with this technique was that it was time-consuming and required a cooperative hoax caller willing to transmit on his or her radio for long periods of time. Unfortunately, most hoax callers made only brief phony calls for help, negating the number of opportunities to mobilize and organize these types of search teams.

The technique was used only on those occasions in which a perpetrator was predictable in his or her calling patterns, such as when a prankster was enamored of a particular female Coast Guard radio watch stander. In these isolated and rare cases, Coast Guard personnel could predict the windows of possibility and develop search teams based on the female watch stander's duty schedule. Knowing the likelihood of the hoax calls enabled shifts of mobile direction-finding teams to be assembled ahead of time.

Improvements at Coast Guard Group Woods Hole would come shortly after the *Sol e Mar* tragedy. New, locally purchased and unique direction-finding equipment would follow, as would equipment and software to help clean up scratchy and garbled recordings of tape recordings of radio calls.

The radio watch standing staff was also doubled in size to permit twelve-hour watches instead of twenty-four-hour shifts. The technology fixes at Woods Hole were stopgap in nature and incomplete primarily because they were unique, one-of-kind and unsupportable in the long term. Unfortunately, due to the various complexities of budgets and politics among several agencies and Congress, it would take almost seven and a half years to finalize plans for Rescue 21. Another tragedy, this time involving the sailing vessel *Morning Dew* (see Chapter 5), again focused attention on the Coast Guard's near-shore technology requirements.

According to the Coast Guard's Rescue 21 website, the 1997 "*Morning Dew* accident validated the need for a new VHF-FM system for the Coast

Guard." We may never know the full story of why it took almost eight more years after the 1990 *Sol e Mar* case and the bellwether *Morning Dew* case for the Coast Guard and Congress to address the technology and coverage problems of its near-shore radio distress system. But the National Transportation Safety Board's (NTSB) 1998 *Morning Dew* report affirmed many of the same technological issues with the radio systems that had affected *Sol e Mar* in 1990.

According to the NTSB's report, "Operational testing on the Direction Finding equipment showed it was inaccurate, had limited features, and thus was not being used. In addition, it could not record the bearing information for later review and correlation to recorded audio transmissions." The NTSB employed U.S. Navy resources and confirmed that "audio recording equipment in use were [*sic*] difficult to operate when searching for specific recorded communications." The recorders "were not suitable for quickly replaying recently received messages."

Today's Coast Guard Rescue 21 system is a combination of audio and digital technologies. Maritime VHF-FM radios purchased in the United States after 1999 are now equipped with both VHF-FM channel 16 (audio), as well as channel 70 (digital) frequencies. One of the huge differences in today's radio systems is the channel 70 or digital select calling (DSC) capability of marine VHF-FM radios.

Distress calls on DSC-equipped marine radios can be activated by the operator with a touch of a button. Moreover, since these radios, if properly registered and connected to the boat's global positioning system, can identify the name of the vessel and its position so rescuers get critical information within a few minutes. The distressed vessel's DSC will stop trying to relay the original distress call if it is acknowledged by the actions of another vessel or a shore station.

Another feature with DSC is that every other sea-based DSC-equipped unit that receives the distressed vessel's transmission will capture the trouble call and could, with operator intervention, then attempt to relay the other boat's distress until acknowledged by a shore-based rescue center.

So in theory, if a modern-day DSC-equipped caller had only four seconds to initiate a Mayday like the *Sol e Mar* did in 1990, the operator conceivably could activate his DSC distress feature on the radio with a touch of a button, using prescripted alerts for a sinking vessel, and then continue to make preparations to abandon ship—and never have to physically talk to anybody. In this example, nearby fishing vessels, if properly equipped with DSC, would have also captured *Sol e Mar*'s DSC distress call and, with their operators' intervention, would have begun to relay the distress call to coastal rescue units, which also could have received the call, either directly or from other relaying vessels.

Additionally, since May 17, 1990, uninspected fishing vessels like *Sol e Mar* have been encouraged to carry satellite emergency position-indicating radio beacons (EPIRBs). EPIRBs, when properly registered and installed, are designed to be activated manually or, if they float free from a sinking vessel, become activated when immersed in salt water and begin transmitting a signal to overhead satellites.

So if the circumstances of the *Sol e Mar* case were to happen today, the Coast Guard's Rescue 21 technology could immediately indicate there were two calls, one from sea and one from land, and provide and record reasonably accurate searchable locations for both transmissions in most locations. And *Sol e Mar*, if equipped, would have had the option to activate its VHF-FM DSC distress function and its onboard satellite EPIRB.

According to Lieutenant Bryan Swintek from Coast Guard Sector Southeast (Group Woods Hole's successor organization):

> *A case like* Sol e Mar *would be treated as distress until we can prove otherwise. If we had two separate calls, we would use R21 to find the lines of bearing* [LOBs] *and see if the calls correlate. Sometimes, we don't get LOBs as the call quality is not "fair." However, we can call the R21 help desk, and they can get a LOB for every call. For any possible hoaxes or cases where we are unsure if there is distress, we make the entire watch listen to the call, we send it to District One* [Boston] *to listen in and then we send it to the SAR Mission Coordinator* [a senior decision-maker] *as well. If anyone thinks it's distress, we treat it as a distress.*

It's also important to note that the Coast Guard had enough technology and information, however flawed, when Billy Hokanson made his Mayday call on March 25, 1990, to begin some type of a rescue operation. The best of any organization's technologies can be nullified if ignored or used improperly.

According to seasoned rescuer Commander Mike DaPonte, "The Coast Guard can have the most up-to-date, most technologically advanced hardware in its command centers that money can buy, but in the end the 'system' remains vulnerable to human error."

8

HUMAN FACTORS AND DECISION MAKING

The early reaction in the aftermath of the March 25, 1990 *Sol e Mar* tragedy was to focus on the Group Woods Hole radio watch stander position. After all, an admiral and two congressmen had seen how this one individual had been overwhelmed by the sheer volume of radio traffic information and other duties on the day of their visit for hearings on July 23, 1990. How could any one person keep up with it all?

And how could watch standers do their jobs, especially if they had to stand twenty-four-hour watches? So additional radio watch standers were assigned to Group Woods Hole after the *Sol e Mar* tragedy to ensure each person stood watches that were no longer than twelve hours.

But the radio watch stander did not make the decision to link Billy Hokanson's legitimate call for help with a later prank call. A more senior Coast Guard decision maker, a group duty officer with, on average, ten to fifteen years of experience, made the fateful decision.

In 1990, the senior decision-making Coast Guard watch standers in the forty-four groups that oversaw search and rescue nationwide were walking an endurance tightrope. A late 1999 fatigue analysis at Group Woods Hole, the same location where tragic errors were made during the *Sol e Mar* case almost a decade before, showed that those senior decision makers were too tired to know they were operating beyond their limits of endurance.

In October 1999, key Coast Guard Group Woods Hole decision makers' sleep and activity indices were being closely monitored as part of a novel analysis when their unit was called on to kick into high gear and respond to the

1999 Egypt Air Flight 990 tragedy. The group operations centers (OPCENs) organized multi-station and multi-unit rescue and law enforcement cases and served as resource brokers, assigning or requesting additional units depending on the complexity of the mission. The groups and their multi-mission rescue stations saved 70 percent of the lives and preserved 90 percent of the property that the entire Coast Guard saved and preserved each year at the time of the study. The pace of operations at Group Woods Hole, Massachusetts, was high throughout the 1990s. On average, 1,250 rescue and 1,500 law enforcement cases occurred within its three-thousand-square-mile area of responsibility each year. From 1998 to 2001, Group Woods Hole and its fourteen subordinate units saved between 60 and 110 people and preserved more than $5 million in property each year. Group Woods Hole was twice at the center of international and national media attention in July 1999, when the small, private airplane owned and operated by John F. Kennedy Jr. crashed seven miles southwest of Martha's Vineyard, and again, on October 31, 1999, when Egypt Air Flight 990 crashed with 217 people on board sixty miles south of Nantucket.

Typically, each group had one senior professional search and rescue–trained Coast Guard petty officer with seven to fifteen years' experience.

Rear Admiral Richard Larrabee, U.S. Coast Guard, incident commander for the JFK Jr. recovery effort, answers questions for the media on July 20, 1999. *Image courtesy of U.S. Coast Guard.*

This officer stood a twenty-four-hour watch and performed a variety of functions from the mundane to the critical, including answering phones, receiving reports of aids to navigation discrepancies, advising the public about navigational aid outages, responding to media queries and coordinating search and rescue cases in response to urgent radio distress calls. This coordination sometimes included lengthy investigative work, the development of search plans, the assignment of appropriate rescue resources, coordination with multiple agencies and comprehensive case documentation. The officers also investigated and determined which cases were real SAR cases and which were hoax or false distress calls, which averaged 30 percent of the SAR case load each year in 1999.

"Normal" watch rotations for these senior watch standers called for twenty-four hours on, followed by seventy-two hours off duty. Although the Coast Guard's policy dictated that these senior personnel maintained a twelve-hour watch, the service also recognized staffing levels were inadequate in 1999 to maintain such a schedule. Because of a lack of adequate staffing, most every group operated with a waiver that authorized the single senior watch stander to stand a twenty-four-hour watch until additional personnel were provided to each unit.

During an average twenty-four-hour duty day, the senior watch stander's duties inhibited regular prolonged sleep and rarely allowed more than four hours of continuous sleep, even during the slowest of workdays. Phones and radio calls occur twenty-four hours a day and often require some degree of analysis beyond the capabilities of the younger, less experienced telecommunications watch standers. Group Woods Hole collaborated with the Coast Guard's Research and Development Center then in Groton, Connecticut, the service's center of excellence for innovative analysis and product development. They identified the need to document the impact of the twenty-four-hour watch schedule on Group Woods Hole's senior watch standers. R&D staff designed a research protocol to monitor the sleep and activity indices of the four senior personnel who stood the twenty-four-hour duty cycle, as well the eight junior telecommunications specialists who stood twelve-hour rotations. The study began in mid-October 1999 and proceeded for a planned thirty-day trial. It was originally designed to capture the impact of the relatively low operations tempo in the fall.

During the study, Group Woods Hole personnel were thrown into the midst of the fast-paced, nationally televised Egypt Air Flight 990 recovery operation on October 31 through November 8, 1999. Thus, the study was able to document sleep and activity profiles from watch standers in both the twelve- and twenty-four-hour watch cycles during a slow-paced environment and during full-scale emergency operations.

The sleep and activity monitoring devices worn by watch standers before, during and after the high-operations tempo periods of the Egypt Air Flight 990 crash response provided a gold mine of information. The information from the R&D Center's analysis conclusively indicated that no watch stander—radio watch stander or the senior watch stander—should ever stand more than twelve hours of watch continuously. The analysis also concluded that personnel who had stood twenty-four-hour shifts were walking a "tightrope" of endurance. After a twenty-four-hour watch, any increase in operational tempo could thrust watch personnel into his or her own personal "red zone" for performance and decision making.

The study concluded that "prolonged performance in the Red Zone will lead to human error and can significantly reduce the safety of Group personnel and the entire maritime community." During the Egypt Air Flight 990 recovery operation, group senior personnel who stood twenty-four-hour cycles often suffered acute periods of suboptimal performance because they were unable to sleep for any period of time. However, the eight junior telecommunications personnel assigned to Group Woods Hole easily transitioned from the low-operations tempo environment to the fast pace of a major disaster's response with no degradation in performance.

The Group Woods Hole–R&D Center study also suggested that each Coast Guard operations center should be staffed with seven senior-level watch standers based on endurance management concepts and the relatively seamless transition made by the eight junior telecommunications watch standers once the Egypt Air Flight 990 disaster response had begun.

Groups Transition to Sectors

In 2006, in the aftermath of 9/11 terrorist attacks and with the addition of numerous homeland security duties, the Coast Guard reorganized its various field units—including the groups—into sector commands. Each sector exercises authority over an assigned area of responsibility. According to the sector organizational manual, "Sectors are commanded by a Commander—typically an officer with the rank of Captain—who exercises the authorities that correspond to the various operational elements combined into Sectors. The Sector Commander is also specifically responsible for overseeing search and rescue (SAR) preparations (including directing SAR-related training exercises), overseeing SAR responses, and making the decision to suspend active SAR searches."

Within each sector, the sector duty officer on duty at any given time "represents the command in all matters pertaining to the Sector and serves as the Sector Commander's direct representative after hours, maintaining a 24x7 watch; this individual has overall responsibility for the entire watch."

The sector command center is also staffed with:

> *A Communications Unit position responsible for monitoring all communications between the Coast Guard and mariners, including receiving calls for assistance from mariners; an Operations Unit position responsible for coordinating or supervising the command and control aspects of all Coast Guard and interagency operations including, but not limited to SAR, Maritime Law Enforcement, Marine Environmental Response, and Ports, Waterways, and Coastal Security missions; a Situation Unit position that is responsible for supervising the command and control aspects of active waterways management and monitoring functions.*

The Coast Guard requires that those who stand watches complete an extensive checklist to show that they have mastered a variety of specific skills that are part of the SAR management process (mastery of each required skill is confirmed by a qualified controller involved in the training process). Trainees are then formally examined by a "qualification board," which typically consists of senior command center leadership and other qualified SAR controllers. Only individuals who have successfully passed the qualification board conduct all prevention and response missions, including SAR cases.

In attempting to characterize the difference between today's sector Operations Centers (OPCENs) and the group OPCENs that existed on March 25, 1990, when the *Sol e Mar* case occurred, 2014 sector commander John Kondratowicz said, "In 1990, you normally had a chief or senior chief supervising both the radiomen and the boatswainmates and quartermasters. Now you have a mid-grade officer, a senior chief petty officer, three operation specialist (OS) chief petty officers, three dedicated civilians and a gaggle of OSs to make up the watch floor. Also on watch you have a minimum of five watch standers compared to two back then." According to Kondratowicz's operations officer, Lieutenant Bryan Swintek, "There is a new standardized national personnel qualification system for each of the four watch positions, and local best practices include monthly SAR operations training, a yearly SAR exercise and monthly Rescue 21 training. And these positions provide several layers of supervision and discussion on cases and 'bench strength' in the event of emergencies. In the past, it was a junior radio watch stander in either an eight- or twelve-hour watch rotation and a senior duty officer, usually in a twenty-four-hour rotation." Captain Kondratowicz went on to indicate that in the modern-day sector OPCEN, "there's never less [sic] than three people on duty at any time on the watch floor."

THE 2009 PATRIOT CASE

But having more operations center watch standers isn't a panacea. And more people with less experience can sometimes create delays in decision making. On January 2, 2009, the fifty-four-foot-long fishing vessel *Patriot*, with Josie Russo's husband, Matteo (thirty-six), and her father, John Orlando (fifty-eight), got underway in the Sector Boston area at about 6:00 p.m., departing from the Gloucester state pier. Matteo and a pregnant Josie, the boat's co-owners, later spoke via cellular telephone between 10:00 and 10:30 p.m. They discussed Matteo's plans to return to the Gloucester state pier the following morning around 10:00 a.m.

At 12:30 a.m., January 3, 2009, the *Patriot* automatically provided its regular vessel monitoring system (VMS) position to government satellites putting the vessel about fourteen and a half miles south-southeast of Gloucester. The VMS was designed to enable the National Marine Fisheries Service and the Coast Guard to ensure fishing vessels operated only in authorized fishing areas. Fishermen had derisively referred to the VMS as their version of "ankle bracelets." For the Coast Guard, this was primarily a law enforcement system.

According to Coast Guard records, the *Patriot*'s in-port automatic fire and intrusion alarm system mysteriously activated at 1:17 a.m. At 1:35 a.m., according to Coast Guard records, Josie Russo first contacted the Coast Guard at Gloucester Station to indicate that the *Patriot*'s remote fire alarm system had been activated. Russo told rescuers that the *Patriot* wasn't supposed to return to the state pier until later that morning and that she had no confirmation that her husband and father had returned, as the alarm may have indicated.

Within fifteen minutes of Mrs. Russo's call, a sleepy watch stander from Coast Guard Station Gloucester requested a VMS "snap shot" (locating position) for the *Patriot* from his senior command, Coast Guard Sector Boston. Shortly after Station Gloucester requested the vessel's VMS position, a review of Coast Guard audio tapes reveal the Sector Boston operations watch stander's frustration with the sector's VMS: "It's not working; it's been down for a week, off and on; I've tried to give it a whirl."

Coast Guard watch standers at three locations debated whether to launch rescue resources for more than three hours despite the possibility that there might be two fishermen in frigid Atlantic waters.

Meanwhile, at 4:34 a.m., an uncorrelated (not registered to a particular vessel) 121.5 MHz "first alert" satellite EPIRB signal was received—the first normal indication of distress in the case. At 4:40 a.m., a Coast Guard Air Station helicopter, now launched and en route to the *Patriot*'s last known VMS position, reported that it was receiving the EPIRB signal on its onboard equipment, indicating it was close to the source of the beacon.

Soon thereafter, rescue units found a debris field, which included the bodies of Russo and Orlando, near the *Patriot*'s last known VMS position.

Vice Admiral R.J. Papp, in charge of the Coast Guard's Atlantic Area, issued his final action in the administrative investigation into the sinking of the fishing vessel *Patriot* on June 11, 2009. Admiral Papp said that "sometime between 1:17 a.m. and 1:30 a.m. [on] January 3, 2009, the fishing vessel PATRIOT…sank approximately 14 nautical miles southeast of Gloucester, Massachusetts." Investigative reports also concluded there was, on average, just one and a half years of search and rescue experience at the sector office during the critical phase of the case.

The Coast Guard's next commandant went on to note, "The fact that both the Sector and District Command Duty Officers were asleep at the time of the incident may have played a role in the relatively inefficient processing and analysis of case information."

Putting the *Sol e Mar* and *Patriot* cases in context, current sector commander Kondratowicz said:

> *We rigorously monitor experience levels in today's operations centers, ensuring there is always an experienced rescue decision maker on watch at all times. We do everything humanly possible to learn from the past and prevent these types of mistakes from ever occurring again. The* Sol e Mar *and* Morning Dew *cases are fine case studies that all operations center personnel and senior leaders go through during their training at SAR school and SAR Supervisors courses. I would be willing to bet in today's era of Rescue 21, these cases would have had a different level of attention by the watchstanders.*

9

CONNECTIONS TO THE PAST

In medical terms, syndactyly is a condition when toes or fingers are fused together at birth. In many ways, the Coast Guard's historic absolute highest and lowest moments were irrevocably fused to the Hokanson family's tragic losses in 1952 and 1990. The previous chapters of this book discuss in detail the sad events surrounding the loss of Hokey and Billy Hokanson on the *Sol e Mar* on the night of March 25, 1990, and the Coast Guard's failure to respond to the boat's distress call due to faulty decision making, a hoax caller and inadequate technology.

But the Hokansons' losses at sea began many years before 1990 in far different and more favorable light in the Coast Guard's history. Sallie Hokanson, Hokey Hokanson's mother, lost her husband, Fritz Hokanson, and her brother Amos Bagge when the fishing vessel *Paolina* sank on February 14, 1952, while en route to New Bedford after a successful fishing trip. *Paolina* had left New Bedford, Massachusetts, on February 6, 1952, to fish in the vicinity of the *Nantucket* lightship. According to *Paolina*'s Coast Guard Marine Board of Investigation, "On 12 February, 1952, the PAOLINA was heard on two occasions by voice radio and its position established as 32 miles south southwest of *Nantucket* Lightship."

Paolina had thirty thousand pounds of mixed fish on board, and the master, Amos Bagge, had expressed his intent to head to New Bedford at midnight to arrive back at home port on the following day, February 13, 1952. The boat was apparently lost at sea and, according to the Coast Guard report, was presumed to have foundered while en route to its home port. Ensign Ben Stabile, later to become the vice commandant of the Coast Guard, recalled how in 1952 his ship, the *Unimak*, along with Coast Guard cutters *Eastwind*, *Legare* and *Acushnet*, was sent to look for *Paolina* and another distressed fishing vessel.

Stabile noted, "*Unimak* was home ported in Boston. At about 2 a.m., I got a recall to the ship for a SAR (search and rescue) case, to search for the missing fishing vessels. Barbara (his wife) took me to the ship and I remember saying, 'Routine SAR will see you in a couple of days' (turned into weeks)."

"We joined a squadron under *Eastwind* with *Legare* and *Frederick Lee*. A bit of debris and a life ring was found after several days of searching. In the meantime the storm came in and the SOS from *Fort Mercer* was received so we were diverted to the datum." (For rescuers, a "datum" is a last-known position.)

According to Stabile, "When our radio gang got the *Ft. Mercer* SOS we turned around in the storm along with *Eastwind* and made slow progress to the reported position, I think the best we could make against the sea and wind was about three knots."

Ben Stabile and many other Coast Guardsmen were underway in their rescue ships at the time the *Fort Mercer*, a 502-foot-long T2 tanker, broke apart forty miles off Cape Cod. Within a few hours of *Fort Mercer*'s distress call, a second 502-foot-long T2 tanker, the *Pendleton*, was found broken in half six miles off Chatham, Massachusetts.

The *Fort Mercer* began to snap apart at around 8:00 a.m. on February 18, 1952. The Coast Guard was well aware of the vessel's problems because its captain had called the night before to indicate he was in trouble. When the moment came when the vessel broke in half, the *Fort Mercer* and the Coast Guard were already on an active communications schedule, providing each other with updates. The captain of the ship had even given an interview to the *Boston Globe* using ship-to-shore radio, updating the public on his vessel's condition before it snapped in two. Some part of the Coast Guard's success in 1952, especially in regards to the thirty-eight seamen rescued from the tank vessel *Fort Mercer*, was in part due to the fact that several rescue vessels were already underway in horrific sea conditions searching for the two missing fishing vessels, including Fritz Hokanson and the fishing vessel *Paolina*.

The cutter *Acushnet*, for example, had been in Portland, Maine, with its engine room torn apart for repairs prior to the *Paolina* rescue call. The *Acushnet* was fully operational, underway and able to perform later heroics because it was out searching for *Paolina* and not disabled by ongoing repairs when the *Fort Mercer*'s later rescue call came in.

The Sol e Mar Tragedy off Martha's Vineyard

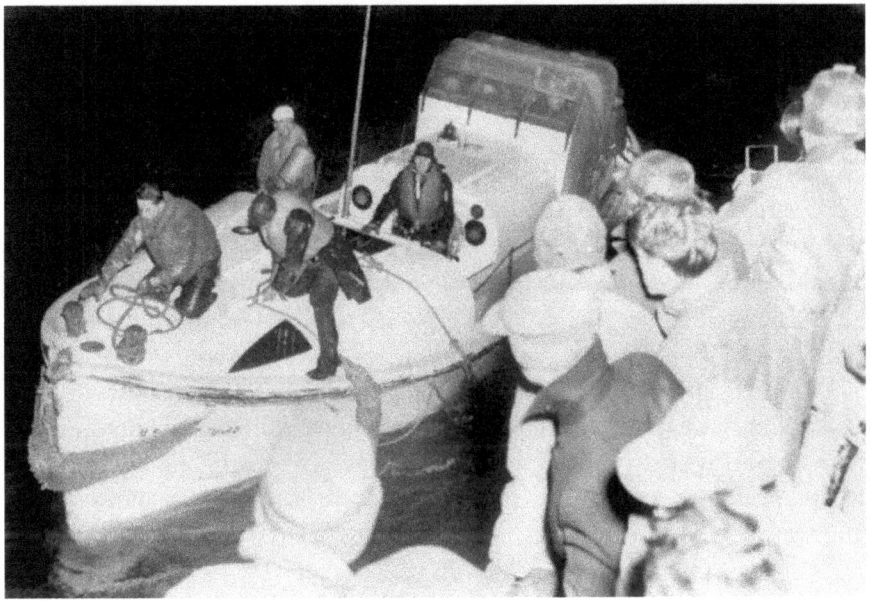

SS *Pendleton* survivors return to Chatham Harbor on February 18, 1952, after being rescued by a thirty-six-foot Coast Guard boat. *Image by Richard C. Kelsey.*

Exhausted SS *Pendleton* survivors. *Image by Richard C. Kelsey.*

The Sol e Mar Tragedy Off Martha's Vineyard

In a 2007 formal message to all Coast Guard members, the commandant highlighted the service's top-ten greatest rescues of all time. The *Pendleton–Fort Mercer* rescues, where 70 of 84 distressed mariners were saved, was formally acknowledged as the Coast Guard's number three all-time most significant rescue effort, behind only the Hurricane Katrina rescues, in which 34,000 lives were saved, and the 1980 liner *Prinsendam* rescue off Alaska, in which 520 were saved.

Few, if any, people acknowledge the unique connectedness the Hokanson family's tragedies have had to the Coast Guard's most significant near-shore rescue event (*Pendleton–Fort Mercer*) and one of its lowest moments (*Sol e Mar*).

Like so many other longtime multigenerational fishing families, the Hokansons have reconciled their painful losses over the past six decades and found new ways to live without their loved ones. No current family members fish other than recreationally. Their pain still stings on certain anniversaries, and tears still flow occasionally for no reason at all.

The Coast Guard celebrates the annual February 18, 1952 anniversary of the *Pendleton–Fort Mercer* heroic rescues at the same time that the Hokansons reflect on a father's and grandfather's passings. Each year, a month or so

PAOLINA 2-14-52
CAPT. ARMAS T. BAGGE
FRITZ HOKANSON
TIMOTHY GUSHUE
HARRY BJUR
WILFRED QUINTIN
HELGER JOHNSON
MARTIN J. BERDINKA
ANNA C. PERRY 3-16-52

Fritz Hokanson's name at New Bedford Seamen's Bethel. *Courtesy of Ellen (Hokanson) Ouellette.*

> KENNETH H. HANSEN
> 1990
> STEVEN J. LAMBERT
> KRISTIAN HAUGE
> "SOL E MAR" 3-25-90
> WM. A. HOKANSON
> WM. A. HOKANSON
> BRADFORD S. CLAPP
> "NEW ENGLAND" 8-28-90
> CARLOS DaCOSTA
> ANTONIO FERNANDES
> ADERITO RIBAU
> "ARISTOCRAT" 9-18-90
> ANDREW NOLAN PARISI

Hokey's and Billy Hokanson's names at New Bedford Seamen's Bethel. *Image courtesy of Ellen (Hokanson) Ouellette.*

after father and grandfather Fritz is remembered by some, Hokey and Billy are recollected by many. And all family members who assisted in the development of this book hope that Hokey and Billy Hokanson's hoax caller someday finds the courage to step forward after twenty-four years and admit his wrongdoing.

POSTSCRIPT

On May 6, 1990, more than five hundred family members and friends bade farewell to Hokey and Billy at the New Bedford Seamen's Bethel, where hundreds of men and boys lost at sea have been eulogized for generations. Reverend Roy Richardson eulogized Hokey and stated, "The smile (painted) on his ship was directly descended from the smile on his face."

Fellow fisherman Mike DeConinck, who used to fish with both Hokansons, had kind words for Billy Hokanson: "Like father, like son—he was all smiles. He always had stories to share, crazy pranks and jokes." Attendees knew that Hokey and Billy had died doing what they loved best. The reverend went on to say, "Hokey loved to sit on the deck of his boat and watch the sun rise. That was his church; that was where he found God."

Those closest to Billy and Hokey knew there was a history of Hokanson family members coming back in dreams and in other ways after their deaths with clues, hints and helpful warnings. Whether this was true or not, and with little empirical evidence to go on, this is what the Hokanson family believed as their truth. Grandfather Fritz Hokanson, who perished in 1952, continued to have a presence with his family long after his death.

Fritz's granddaughter Cheryl Best recounted a story her grandmother Sallie told her about him. Setting the tone for the anecdote, Best described her grandmother: "She was a no-nonsense kind of woman, not given to tell[ing] tales. She never gossiped or lied and had an inner peace." Best went on to describe how Sallie explained how Fritz would come home from his

POSTSCRIPT

Sol e Mar passing through the New Bedford hurricane barrier with Hokey's happy face painted on the hull. Billy Hokanson is standing just outside the wheelhouse. *Image courtesy of Mr. John Ryan.*

```
                    Seamen's Bethel
                    Memorial Service
                          for
                   William A. Hokanson
                           &                                    "DONATIONS"
                  William A. Hokanson Jr.
                      May 6, 1990            Donations can be made to the:
                                                    William A. Hokanson Jr.
                                                        Scholarship Fund
The Word of Grace                                             for
Greeting                                       New Bedford Vocational High School
Prayer                                                  Marine Industries
Eulogy........................Mike DeConnick
                              Ricky Oliveria       c/o Fairhaven Savings Bank
                              Randy Oliveria

Song: Free Bird
Afternoon Scripture                         You are all invited to a colation immediately
Afternoon Message                                   following at the home of:

A Letter For Dad...............Cheryl Best           Mr. & Mrs. Wayne Ford
                                                        168 N. Main St.
Prayer                                                   Acushnet, Ma.

Lord's Prayer (in unison)                   Parking available in St. Francis Church lot.

A Poem........................Kerri Rassmusen

Reading of 23rd Psalm

Song: You are the wind beneath my wings
          sung by: Sharon Lainey Tavares

Prayers

Benediction
```

Hokey and Billy's memorial service program, May 6, 1990. *Image courtesy of Ellen (Hokanson) Ouellette.*

fishing trips and sit in a rocking chair and smoke a cigar. Sallie told Best that there were times after his death that she smelled his cigar and saw the chair rocking by itself.

Years later, Best told Randy Oliveira the story Grandmother Sallie had told her about her grandfather's ethereal presence and the cigar. To Best's surprise, Randy named the type of cigar her grandfather smoked. "How did you know that?" inquired Best. Randy explained that Hokey "had told me he had the same experience with his father's cigar smell and the rocking chair when visiting his mother."

Hokey's dead father, Fritz, would also appear in Hokey's dreams to forewarn him of imminent danger. Once, Hokey had been fishing by himself. He had been hurt and was taking a nap after putting the boat on autopilot. According to several family members, "Hokey reported that his father had come to him in his dream and told him to wake up—danger was close!" Hokey somehow awoke and found that his boat was about to ram an offshore weather buoy. But thanks to the dream warning, he was able to avoid a catastrophe.

In a final message to his son from beyond, Fritz warned Hokey in a vision not to return to the hard life of fishing lest he become a victim of nature's fury before his forty-fifth birthday. Hokey's daughter, Cheryl Best, recounts how "Hokey told me he saw something out of the side of his eye towards *Sol e Mar*'s stern area. When Hokey went aft, he saw and spoke to his father, Fritz, who gave him the final warning."

Best, who had just received her insurance license in March 1990, called her father, Hokey, on the boat's cellphone while he was underway on his last fateful trip. She offered to write him a policy to mitigate the prophecy. True to form, Hokey shrugged off his daughter's offer and cast his fate to the sea. For unknown reasons, Best "broke down and cried uncontrollably after she hung up the phone with her father. I knew that would be the last time we ever talked." Hokey perished with his son, Billy Hokanson, the night of March 25, 1990, just prior to Hokey's forty-fifth birthday.

According to Hokey's ex-wife, Ellen Ouellette:

> *The Christmas before he died, Billy came home and gave me a handful of dollar bills. I asked him what they were for, and he said, "Dad said to give this to you." I said "No, I don't want or need his money, give it back to him." Billy said, "No, he said, 'Merry Christmas' and to give them to you." They were all crumpled up, which they always were in Hokey's pocket. When I counted them, there was $44.00. It was like he was telling*

Postscript

me something about him not seeing forty-five...I still remember that day like it was yesterday.

Ellen Ouellette also had an odd dream just before the tragedy:

I had a dream a few nights before the boat went down. Ed [her husband] was working 11:00 p.m. to 7:00 a.m., and I was home alone. I dreamt the phone rang, and it was Billy. He said he was stuck, and he ran out of gas. I kept asking him where he was, but he never answered me. And then he hung up—it seemed so real I actually called Ed at work and asked him what to do. He said call the phone company, and maybe they could trace the call. I did. They said no call came in to our phone. I couldn't get back to sleep. The next morning, I called Billy and asked him if he called me. He said, "No." He came for supper. He and Ed really teased me about it. Ed asked Billy if he needed a few dimes for the phone booth so he could call and check in with me.

Years after his 1990 death, young Billy Hokanson would repeatedly visit his sister, Cheryl Best, in her dreams. Here, Billy guided Cheryl to reach out to his cousin Randy Oliveira. Both Randy and Cheryl were recovering from difficult circumstances at the time. She was going through an eight-month recovery from leg surgery and the demons of drugs and alcohol. Randy had been consumed by opiates, painkillers and steroids—the products of years of contact-sport injuries. He had lost forty pounds from his rugged athletic frame as a result of being an addict.

Cheryl followed her brother's advice and contacted Randy. They arranged a meeting at the Fort Phoenix Overlook, the same location that her father, Hokey, and his brothers had been brought to in 1952 in order to fruitlessly wait for Fritz Hokanson's return. The reunion between Cheryl and Randy reignited a forgotten flame, and the two renewed a lost romance. As of this writing, they are living happily together on Martha's Vineyard.

In another eerie circumstance, Billy Hokanson would return to invade his sister Cheryl Best's dreams, this time, guiding her to render aid to a Martha's Vineyard neighbor in financial distress. Making the dream more spectacular was the fact that Billy Hokanson could not have known Cheryl's neighbor, since Cheryl had not befriended or even known the neighbor until after Billy's death.

Keeping her brother's advocacy about the neighbor to herself, Cheryl was stunned the next day when the neighbor called Cheryl's place of work,

POSTSCRIPT

Randy Oliveira and Cheryl Best outside a Martha's Vineyard restaurant, October 2013. *Authors' collection.*

a septic company, seeking relief from regular payments for services. The woman could not afford a new septic system and had to have her system repeatedly pumped out. At this point, Cheryl petitioned her boss with her brother's message from beyond, and Cheryl and her boss assisted the neighbor in several ways.

Billy would also, according to Aunt Joyce Oliveira, sometimes visit her in her twilight wakening state, and she swears she has heard his familiar "Auntie" greeting. Besides family dreams and visions, Hokey and Billy's impact persists well beyond their passing.

There was no denying the longevity of Hokey's and Billy's magnetism with women, including Hokey's last girlfriend, Jeannie Berberian. Despite the passage of time and a new husband, Jeannie memorialized her relationship with Hokey and Billy eight years after their deaths with a permanent tattoo. Berberian spent "six hundred dollars to emboss an image of the *Sol e Mar*, Hokey and Billy and their two dogs on her back."

Jeannie also insists she has seen the beloved and departed fishermen in her dreams, "riding majestically in a pristine *Sol e Mar*, happy as ever."

Postscript

Jeannie Berberian's full-length back tattoo memorializing Billy, Hokey and their two dogs. *Image courtesy of Jeannie Berberian.*

Billy's mother, Ellen, the main advocate and champion for the various government investigations in the aftermath of the *Sol e Mar* sinking and for the publication of this book, now lives quietly on Billy's Way in Fairhaven, Massachusetts, with husband Eddie Ouellette. Ellen and Eddie tell the story of the road they live on and how it came to be renamed Billy's Way as part of a 9-1-1 rezoning plan for the town. When she and neighbors were told they would have to come up with suggestions for a new name, the girl who was administering the process said, "Why don't you name it Billy's Way?" The girl had known Billy years before and had admired him. Ellen and Eddie's home on Billy's Way looks over the entrance to Fairhaven Harbor and faces the Fort Phoenix Overlook, and they watch the fishing boats come and go.

According to Ellen, "I got a tattoo two years after the sinking—one red rose with Billy's name on it. It is on my left chest, on my heart." Her music box sometimes plays for no reason, and she sees "shadows walking around the living room at night after I go to bed." Ellen knows "he [Billy] is around me all the time. I have a bandanna that Billy had on in a picture

Postscript

Billy's Way street sign. *Authors' collection.*

tied to my bed post. I hold it every night when I fall asleep. It's like I am holding him."

Like so many families after tragedy, the Hokansons, Ouellettes and Oliveiras were all adversely affected in different ways after the sinking and loss of their beloved Hokey and Billy. But today, with the passage of time and an abundance of effort, most of the families and friends have reconciled their losses. They have certainly not forgotten the tragedy, but many celebrated the 2013 holiday season together for the first time in several years.

When asked what each of them would do if they found out who the hoax caller was, their answers were consistently reflective of their personalities. Billy's cousin and *Sol e Mar* crewmate Randy Oliveira stated, "I would be afraid for what I might do to the person." Billy's sister, Cheryl, "isn't sure that the hoax caller knew what they had done at the time, but [I] hope that he would apologize." Hokey's ex-wife and Billy's mother, Ellen Ouellette, hopes "lessons are learned and this never happens again."

BIBLIOGRAPHY

Alfred, G. "F/V *Sol E Mar* Sinking in the North Atlantic Ocean in Position 41-07.7n, 070-45.0w on March 25, 1990, Resulting in the Missing and Presumed Death of Mr. William Arthur Hokanson Sr. and Mr. William Arthur Hokanson Jr." Marine Safety Office Providence letter 16732, dated July 10, 1990.

Astley, John. Interview by authors. Cape Elizabeth, ME, January 22, 2014.

Berberian, Jeannie. Phone interview by authors. Cape Elizabeth, ME, November 8, 2013.

Best, Cheryl. Interview by authors. Martha's Vineyard, MA, October 31, 2013.

Best, Cheryl, to commander, Coast Guard Group Woods Hole, August 17, 1992.

Boyle, Maureen. "A Year Later, What Have We Learned from *Sol e Mar*?" *(New Bedford, MA) Barnacle*, May 24, 1991.

Breazeale, Dr. Ron. E-mail interview by authors. Cape Elizabeth, ME, November 21, 2013.

Butcher, Dave. Phone interview by authors. Cape Elizabeth, ME, November 3, 2013.

Casto, R.J., rear admiral, chief acquisitions officer, U.S. Coast Guard. ALCOAST service-wide message to the Coast Guard. Subject: NDSMP; dated March 2000.

"The Coast Guard's Auxiliary, Volunteer Arm of America's Premier Maritime Service." U.S. Coast Guard History. http://www.uscg.mil/history/articles/cgauxiliary.pdf (accessed June 5, 2014).

BIBLIOGRAPHY

Commander, Coast Guard Group Woods Hole, to Cheryl Best, August 28, 1992.

Commander, Coast Guard Group Woods Hole. Letter 1330: Personnel Allowance Amendment (PAA) Request. March 8, 1999.

———. Letter 1330. August 15, 2000.

Commander, First Coast Guard District. Letter 5312: Watch Duty Length at Group/Activity Command Centers and Communications Centers. July 21, 2000.

Commercial Fisheries News. "*Sol e Mar* Prompts Hoax Legislation." September 1, 1990.

Couto, Lucinda. "Defying Danger, Fishermen Died as They Lived." *(New Bedford, MA) Standard Times*, May 7, 1990.

Daponte, CDR Mike. E-mail interview by authors. Cape Elizabeth, ME, November 15, 2013.

Dave, Dutra. Phone interview by authors. Cape Elizabeth, ME, December 7, 2013.

David, Beth. "Sea Lure Meets Sea Lore." *Fairhaven Neighborhood News*, April 13, 2006.

Davis, Franny. E-mail interview by authors. Cape Elizabeth, ME, December 15, 2013.

DeConinck, Mike. Interview by authors. Cape Elizabeth, ME, January 15, 2014.

Dobnik, Verona. "Hoax Sea Emergencies Cost Coast Guard, Taxpayers." Associated Press Worldstream, June 12, 2012.

Dunlop, Thomas. "The Defection of Simas Kadurkis." *Martha's Vineyard Magazine* (Summer 2005).

Francis, Dave. E-mail interview by authors. Cape Elizabeth, ME, December 6, 2013.

Grant, Traci. "Bodies of Burn Victim, Passenger Recovered in Maine Copter Crash." *Boston Globe*, November 24, 1993.

Hiscock, Richard. E-mail interview by authors. Cape Elizabeth, ME, October 21, 2013.

Isoardi, Katherine. "Optimizing the Appropriate Use of the Emergency Call System, and Dealing with Hoax Callers." *Emergency Medicine*, November 10, 2010.

Kondratowicz, Captain John. E-mail interview by authors. Cape Elizabeth, ME, March 31, 2014.

Lakshamanan, Indira. "Search for Medical Helicopter Down in Casco Bay." *Boston Globe*, November 20, 1993.

Bibliography

Loy, Admiral James. "Lessons Learned from *Morning Dew*, Remarks at the U.S. Naval Institute's 125th Annual Meeting at the U.S. Naval Academy, April 22, 1999." *U.S. Naval Institute Proceedings*, June 1, 1999.

Lumb, Dr. Richard. E-mail interview by authors. Cape Elizabeth, ME, November 25, 2013.

Lynch, Don. E-mail interview by authors. Cape Elizabeth, ME, November 5, 2013.

Marine Accident Report NTSB/MAR-99/01. *Sinking of the Recreational Sailing Vessel* Morning Dew *at the Entrance to the Harbor of Charleston, South Carolina*. December 29, 1997.

Mokry, Joe. Interview by authors. Cape Elizabeth, ME, November 6, 2013.

(New Bedford, MA) Barnacle. "Interview of Congressman Gerry Studds." March 21, 1991.

Office of Technology Assessment. *Biological Rhythms: Implications for the Worker*. Report OTA-BA-463. Washington, D.C.: U.S. Government Printing Office, 1991.

Oliveira, Joyce, and Ray Oliveira. Interview by authors. Fairhaven, MA, November 1, 2013.

Oliveira, Randy. Interview by authors. Martha's Vineyard, MA, October 31, 2013.

Oliveira, Ray. "Last Words." *Contractor Connection*, April 15, 1996.

Ouellette, Eddie. Interview by authors. Fairhaven, MA, November 1, 2013.

Ouellette, Ellen (Hokanson). E-mail interview by authors. Cape Elizabeth, ME, December 14, 2013.

———. Handwritten notes. From Captain Bud Breault, USCG (Ret.), former chief of Search and Rescue, First Coast Guard District–Boston at the time of the sinking, April 1990.

———. Personal journal entries for March–July 1990.

Raposo, Saul. Phone interview by authors. Cape Elizabeth, ME, December 2, 2013.

"Registration Successful!" Prankdial. http://www.prankdial.com/browse (accessed June 5, 2014).

"Remarkable Recovery of Seven-Year-Old." Sveriges Radio. http://sverigesradio.se/sida/artikel.aspx?Programid=2054&artikel=4296666 (accessed March 16, 2014).

"Rescue 21." USCG. http://www.uscg.mil/acquisition/rescue21/ (accessed June 5, 2014).

Rybacki, Admiral Richard, USCG. "Admiral Sheds Light on *Sol e Mar* Investigation." *Commercial Fisheries News*, June 1, 1990.

BIBLIOGRAPHY

———. "Informal Search and Rescue Case Study and Claims Litigation Investigation into the Circumstances Surrounding the Fishing Vessel *Sol e Mar* Reported Overdue on 30 March 1990 in the Waters South of Nomans Island." July 11, 1990.

"Search and Rescue Is NO JOKE!" USCG Office of Search & Rescue (CG-534). http://www.uscg.mil/hq/cg5/cg534/sarfactsinfo/sarisnojoke.asp (accessed January 12, 2014).

Searles, Dick. Phone interview by authors. Cape Elizabeth, ME, January 12, 2014.

Smith, Richard, FCC. "Testimony to the House Sub-Committee of on Coast Guard and Navigation, July 23, 1990." Author's personal collection.

Smith, Dr. Peter. Interview by authors. Cape Elizabeth, ME, November 6, 2013.

Stancliff, Sherry. "The Fort Mercer and Pendleton Rescues." U.S. Coast Guard History. http://www.uscg.mil/history/articles/Pendleton_Mercer_Stancliff.asp (accessed June 5, 2014).

Steinman, Admiral Al. E-mail interview by authors. Cape Elizabeth, ME, November 15, 2013.

Swintek, Bryan. E-mail interview by author. Cape Elizabeth, ME, March 31, 2014.

U.S. Coast Guard Addendum to the United States National Search and Rescue Supplement (NSS) to the International Aeronautical and Maritime Search and Rescue Manual (IAMSAR). COMDT Instruction M16130.2E. September 2009.

U.S. Coast Guard Instruction M16501.6. "Operational Mission Performance Expectations: Groups, Stations, Aids to Navigation Teams." November 13, 2000.

U.S. Coast Guard Marine Board of Investigation. Investigation of the sinking of the fishing vessel *Paolina*, June 16, 1952.

U.S. Coast Guard Record Message. "Interim Policy for Watch Duty Length at Group/Activity Command Centers and Communications Centers." ALDIST 209/99, 071434Z, June 1999.

———. "Policy for Watch Duty Length at Coast Guard Command Centers." ALCOAST 163/01, 111910Z, April 2001,

U.S. Coast Guard Station Menemsha, Martha's Vineyard. Unit log, April 1, 1990.

"What Is FOIA?" FOIA.gov. http://www.foia.gov/about.html (accessed March 16, 2014).

Wikipedia. "List of Walt Disney Pictures films." http://en.wikipedia.org/wiki/List_of_Walt_Disney_Pictures_films (accessed June 4, 2014).

INDEX

A

Acushnet 106
Air Med 37
AK47 25
annual State of the
　Coast Guard
　address 89
antisocial personality
　disorder 41
Astley, John Captain 86
Atlantic Ocean
　claiming lives 51
　forty-three degrees 66
Australia 42

B

Bagge, Amos 105
Bagge, Barbara 106
Barnacle 71
Berberian, Jeannie 16,
　31, 115
Best, Cheryl 10, 12, 15,
　26, 27, 76, 77,
　111, 113, 114
Best, Scott 26
Billy's Way 116

body immersion into
　cold water
　physical reactions to 67
Boston Harbor 22
Boston, Massachusetts
　16, 19, 20, 22, 24,
　37, 39, 40, 46, 50,
　64, 72, 84, 86, 95,
　102, 103, 106
Boston's Pier 7 19, 46
Bova, Michael 84
Bradford, Robert
　CGPO 82
Brant Point, Nantucket
　CG Rescue Station
　48, 91
Butcher, Dave 15, 22,
　33, 47, 58, 72

C

Canal Point, Florida 79
Cape Elizabeth, Maine 37
Carver, Massachusetts 24
Casco Bay, Maine 17,
　37, 38, 39
Casto, Admiral R.J. 90

channel 9 66
channel 16 38, 66, 94
Chappaquiddick Island 34
Charleston, South
　Carolina 78
Chilmark 34
Coast Guard
　collection of prank
　calls 81
　cutter crew 34
　distress call response
　failure 105
　EPIRB distress signal 62
　near-shore radio
　distress system 90
　onslaught of hoax
　callers 87
　potential liability 76
　rescue helicopters and
　boats 61
　rescuers 20
　utility boat 84
　weekly calls for help 82
Coast Guard Air Station,
　Cape Cod 50, 51
Coast Guard Group
　Portland 38

INDEX

Coast Guard Group Woods Hole improvements 93
Coast Guard Reserve Act of 1939 92
Coast Guard's Atlantic Area 103
Coast Guard's Marine Safety Office 59
Coast Guard's Research and Development Center Groton, Connecticut 99
cold shock
  body's reaction to water 67
  two-minute critical period 67
Commercial Fisheries News 64
  article, *Sol e Mar* 65
Cornett, Daniel 78
Cornett, Libby 79
Cornett, Michael 78
Cornett, Paul 78
Cortez, Daniel 82
Cuttyhunk Island 48
  marine salvage operator 51

D

DaPonte, Commander Mike 70
  seasoned rescuer 95
datum
  "last known position" 106
David, Beth 54
Davis, Francis "Franny" 16, 24, 58
DeConinck, Helen 26
DeConinck, Mike 18, 26, 32, 33, 53, 55, 57, 59, 111
digital select calling (DSC) 94

District SAR (search and rescue) plan 70
Dutra, Dave 16, 22, 26

E

East Sullivan, Maine 37
Eastwind 106
Egypt Air Flight 990 98
  October 1999 crash 98
emergency beacon 62
Emergency Position Indicating Radio Beacon (EPIRB) 61
  received in the *Patriot* case 103

F

Fairhaven Neighborhood News 54
FCC 41, 86
Fernald, Douglas 37
flounder 47
Forest, Mark 82
Fort Mercer 106
Fort Phoenix Overlook 114
Frederick Lee 106
Freedom of Information Act (FOIA) 77

G

gasp reflex 67
Gay Head, Martha's Vineyard 51
Gloucester 102
Gloucester state pier 102
Good Sam's 38
Green, Lieutenant Jerry 38
group duty officer 97
Group Operations Centers (OPCENs) 98

Group Portland (Maine) Group Duty Officer 70
Group Woods Hole Operations Center 48
Group Woods Hole–R&D Center study 100

H

harbor seal 54
Hiscock, Richard
  exposure suits 60
  fishing vessel safety advocate 60
hoax calls
  1990 81
Hoax emergency calls
  cost to taypayers 85
Hokanson
  family tragedies 108
Hokanson, Billy 19
  1990 distress call 91
  distress call 44
  garbled cry for help 65
  intelligence 28
  kind words 111
  nickname 27
  physical characteristics 31
  prankster at large 40
  presumed lost 53
  visitations 114
Hokanson family members
  presence at hearing 75
Hokanson, Fritz
  1952 death 45
Hokanson, Hokey
  avid reader 26
  fatherhood 26
  gun collector 24
  lack of verifying vessel stability 60

124

Index

lost skipper 53
love of animals 24
physical characteristics 21
storage of emergency gear 63
Hokanson, Sallie 23, 105
Hokanson, William "Hokey" 19
Hokey II 28
H.R. 4632 71
Hurd, Bobby, Jr. 78
Hurricane Katrina 108
hypothermia 37
 beginning of cooling 68
 concerns 66

I

Island Holiday 38
Isoardi, Katherine 42

J

Jaws 34
Jeton, Matthew T. 37
Juvenile Justice and Delinquency Prevention Act 86

K

Kadurka, Simas 34
Kelly's Boat Yard, Fairhaven, Massachusetts 50
Kennedy, John F., Jr.
 July 1999 crash 98
Kennedy, U.S. senator Edward M. "Ted" 34
Kondratowicz, Captain John
 sector commander 16, 101, 103

L

Landvogt, Tom 77
Legare 106
LEOs 40
Linberg, Jeff
 owner, Linberg Marine, Inc. 16, 53, 57
lines of bearing (LOBs) 95
Litva 34
Lobster Bowl restaurant 20
Long Island Sound 50
Loy, Commandant James 89
Ludington, Ohio News 82
Lumb, Dr. Richard 43
Lynch, Don 48

M

Maersk Alabama 69
Magnuson Fisheries Conservation Law 83
Maine Marine Patrol 38
Maine Medical Center 37
Margaret Marie 82
Marlin 53, 54, 55, 57, 59, 73
Martha's Vineyard 7, 10, 11, 13, 19, 27, 34, 48, 50, 51, 53, 62, 66, 72, 73, 91, 114
 search area 50
mass casualty incident 85
Max 19, 31, 51, 58, 60
Mayday 51
McIntyre, Donald M. 37
Menemsha 34
Menemsha Bight 34
Menemsha Harbor 34
Menemsha Station 49

Messecar, Michael 84
Millpoint 32
Minflicka 65
Mirachi, Frank 65
Miss Teen USA 22
Mokry, Joe 39
Morning Dew 78
 loss in 1997 78

N

Nantucket 10, 24, 45, 48, 50, 65, 66, 72, 76, 91, 98, 105
Nantucket lightship 45
National Distress and System Modernization Program (NDSMP) 90
National Distress System (NDS) 81
National Marine Fisheries Service 102
National Search and Rescue Addendum 75
New Bedford, Massachusetts 26, 28, 73, 75, 81, 105, 111
New Bedford Vocational Technical High School 28
next of kin (NOK) 75
9/11 terrorist attacks 41
 2006, in the aftermath of 100
Nintendo 30
Nomans Island 11, 24, 48, 76, 91

O

Oliveira, Joyce 15, 19, 23, 29, 115

125

INDEX

Oliveira, Randy 15, 24, 25, 27, 28, 34, 63, 113, 114, 117
Oliveira, Ray 19
Oliveira, Ricky 29
Orlando, John 102
Otterlind, Dr. 68
Ouellette, Eddie 15, 21, 28, 31, 116
Ouellette, Ellen (Hokanson) 23, 24, 26, 27, 31, 50, 58, 59, 65, 66, 76, 77, 113, 114, 116, 117
   tattoos 116
oxygen/acetylene cutting torch 57

P

packing gland 59
Paolina 45, 46, 105, 106
   1952 sinking 105
Papp, Vice Admiral R.J. 103
paravane
   water kite 47
Patriot 102
Pearl Ace 78
Pendleton 106
Personal Flotation Devices (PFD) 62
Pettit, Captain Anthony 65
Phillips, Captain Rich 69
Plymouth, Massachusetts 24
prankcall.com 43
Prinsendam 108

Q

Queensland Ambulance Service 42
Quissett Harbor 67

R

radio "dead zone" 49
Rafter, John "Sean" 37
Raposo, Saul 26, 29
Rasmussen, Kerri 47
remotely operated vehicle 54
Rescue 21 11, 12, 85, 90, 91, 93, 94, 95, 102, 103
Resolute 15, 33, 47, 48, 50, 51, 53, 55, 58, 60, 65, 66, 72, 73
Richardson, Reverend Roy 111
ROV video screen 55
Ruksenas, Algis 34
Russo, Josie 102
Russo, Matteo 102
Rybacki, Richard, Rear Admiral
   issued findings 63
Rybacki, Rich Rear Admiral 48, 75

S

sand dabs 26
Sandy Hook, New Jersey 85
SAR management process
   CG-required skills 101
SDO (senior duty officer) 63
SEAL Team 6 69
Seamen's Bethel 111
Search and Rescue
   Coast Guard petty officers 98
Searles, Dick 54
Sea Tow 48
Sector Command Center
   staffing positions and specialities 101

sector commands
   CG Commands 100
Skipper Motor Inn 65
Smith, Peter 40
Smith, Richard 85
Snoopy 19, 51, 58, 60
Sol e Mar
   at anchor 57
   conversion to dragger 59
   crew 30
   crewman 25
   cruel prank 81
   departure from Fairhaven 60
   discovery of 55
   emergency equipment 61
   final trip 46
   fishing vessel 19
   freeing ports 60
   friends' search 53
   geographic position 48
   hoax caller 44
   immediate aftermath 97
   immersion suit 62
   lack of safety drills 63
   length 45
   location of distress call 50
   mast 34
   notoriety 82
   official congressional hearings 71
   operational and legal issues 63
   outriggers 47
   overdue 50
   pilot house 26
   role of weather 57
   search suspended 51
   SOS 48
   survival suit 51
   technology and human failures 92
   ten years after sinking 89

INDEX

Southern Maine EMS 40
Southern Maine
   EMS Critical
   Incident Stress
   Management
   team 41
Stabile, Ben Ensign 106
Stamford, Connecticut
   Police 84
Steinman, Al 67
Studds Act 84
Studds, Congressman
   Gerry 71
Subcommittee on
   Coast Guard
   and Navigation,
   Committee on
   Merchant Marine
   and Fisheries 71
Swintek, Lieutenant
   Bryan 95
syndactyly 105

T

Tausin, Congressman
   Billy 71
taxpayers
   cost of hoax calls 82
Toms River, New Jersey
   39
Turks and Caicos
   Islands 84

U

Unimak 106
University of New
   England 43
Urgent Marine
   Information
   Broadcast
   (UMIB) 51
U.S. Attorney's Office 86

U.S. Naval Academy,
   Annapolis,
   Maryland 89
U.S. Navy attack
   submarine
   theory of *Sol e Mar*
   sinking 58

V

Vaill Island 39
vessel monitoring system
   (VMS) 102
Viking heritage 30

W

Waldschmidt, Dan CWO
   82
watch standers
   Coast Guard 103
   Group Charleston 78
   Group Woods Hole
      12, 50, 63, 64,
      70, 81, 89, 90,
      97, 99, 103
Morning Dew case 78
radio operators 78
Sector Boston 102
Water Extrication Team
   (WET) 37
wind and tidal currents 53
Woods Hole
   Oceanographic
   Institute 71

ABOUT THE AUTHORS

Captain W. Russell Webster, U.S. Coast Guard (Ret.), is the former Coast Guard Group Woods Hole commander and a Coast Guard historian who writes and lectures on historical and contemporary rescue cases.

Captain Webster was formally recognized in 2010 by the Coast Guard's former commandant Thad Allen and the Foundation for Coast Guard History and then again in 2012 by the First Coast Guard District commander Rear Admiral Dan Neptun with acknowledgements and public service commendations for his "30 years as a strong proponent of capturing and interpreting service history."

Elizabeth Webster and Captain W. Russ Webster, USCG (Ret.). *Courtesy Andrew Webster.*

This is his third book. He has coauthored *The Pendleton Disaster Off Cape Cod: The Greatest Small Boat Rescue in Coast Guard History* and the children's version of that iconic 1952 mission, *The Daring Coast Guard Rescue of the Pendleton Crew*, with Theresa Mitchell Barbo.

Elizabeth Webster has been a freelance journalist for more than thirty years for Maine's three major newspapers: the *Bangor Daily News*, the *Lewiston Sun Journal* and the *Portland Press Herald*. This is her first book.

www.ingramcontent.com/pod-product-compliance
Lightning Source LLC
Chambersburg PA
CBHW060812100426
42813CB00004B/1045